Cantigny Conference Series
Conference Report

The Military, The Media and The Administration: An Irregular Triangle

Nancy Ethiel, Editor

Sponsored by the McCormick Tribune Foundation

The Military, The Media and The Administration: An Irregular Triangle

Published by the
McCormick Tribune Foundation
435 North Michigan Avenue
Suite 770
Chicago, Illinois 60611
312/222-3512
E-mail: rrmtf@tribune.com

The Military, The Media and The Administration: An Irregular Triangle

Table of Contents

Foreword

From its inception in 1992, the McCormick Tribune Foundation's military-media conference series has provided a neutral forum in which journalists and military officers discuss the issues that unavoidably arise from their very dissimilar roles in defending America's freedoms.

The sixth conference in this series, in August 2001, highlighted two enduring sources of tension—military investigations and the effect of civilian leadership on the military-media relationship. Meeting at Cantigny, the foundation's estate just outside Chicago, representatives of the military and the media had the opportunity to express their disparate obligations, establish trust in each other, and develop channels of communication in a time of peace. This report is an account of their conversations.

Of course, the shattering events that occurred soon after the conference once again put their complicated but essential relationship to the test. Because of those events, some of the specifics discussed at the conference have become moot, or have moved to the background. The Quadrennial Defense Review (QDR), much on the minds of conferees, has taken a back seat to the war on terrorism, for example. But the concerns both military and media had then about the Bush administration's penchant for secrecy have only been amplified. The administration continues to exercise unusually tight control over the flow of information about and access to the war on terrorism. In addition, the concerns expressed at the conference about the need to understand the special nature of the military justice system have taken on new meaning and urgency, as the administration has indicated it may try alleged terrorists in military, not civilian, courts.

To bring the issues conferees discussed into current focus, this report includes three essays about the military-media relationship in the wake of Sept. 11, from the perspectives of the military, the media and the civilian leadership.

All of the Cantigny conferees made valuable contributions to this important discussion, but special thanks go to Harry Disch, president of the Center for Media and Security Ltd., who organized the conference for the foundation, and to Washington lawyer Jeffrey Smith of Arnold & Porter, who moderated the conference sessions.

It is our hope that the expert presentations, rich discussions, and well-informed observations of our Cantigny conferees will prove to be as valuable to readers of this report as they were to those who attended.

Richard A. Behrenhausen
President and Chief Executive Officer
McCormick Tribune Foundation

Chapter 1
The Irregular Triangle: A Taxonomy of Civil-Military-Media Relations

Past Cantigny conferences have focused primarily on the relationship and the frictions between the military and the media. But considering this as only a two-sided dialogue ignores an important dimension: the effect of civilian leadership. To address the interplay between civilian leadership, the military, and the media when it comes to informing the public about national security issues, the foundation commissioned a paper by noted scholar Andrew Bacevich, professor of international relations at Boston University. His paper, which follows, formed the basis for much discussion at the conference.

An abiding myth of our time is that fractious relations among the government, military services, and the media are largely an outgrowth of the various events—beginning with the Bay of Pigs, continuing through Vietnam, and culminating with Watergate—that get lumped together under the rubric of "the sixties." In other words, the phenomenon is relatively recent and, if not uniquely American, at least afflicts the United States to a far greater extent than other nations. However, this myth does not stand up even to casual scrutiny. Conflict among political authorities, military institutions, and the press long predates the 1960s. Nor is the phenomenon one that makes itself felt particularly in the United States.

Consider: in 1854, William Howard Russell, a correspondent covering the Crimean War for the *London Times*, penned a series of voluminous dispatches taking the British command to task for its multiple failures. In great and excruciating detail, Russell recounted at first hand the travails of troops, who were ill-clothed and ill-fed, and who died of disease in appalling numbers. He described the very different lot of callous and stupid generals enjoying pampered lives. He depicted the professional incompetence that led to pointless slaughter in actions such as the charge of the Light Brigade. Critics cried treason: Russell was undermining morale and giving aid and comfort to Britain's enemies. But at home his reports roused a storm of popular indignation. In the end, Russell's revelations were credited with toppling the government of then Prime Minister Lord Aberdeen. A new cabinet took power with a mandate to implement vitally needed military reforms. Russell had "saved the army from annihilation through sheer neglect," said Nicholas Bentley in his introduction to the 1967 edition of *Russell's Dispatches from the Crimea, 1854-1856*. Whatever the merit of that claim, Russell had unquestionably made himself the beau ideal of a war correspondent, after which many others would model themselves.

Or consider the venomous relationship between the press and William T. Sherman during the Civil War. If ever there was a worthy cause, preserving the union and bringing an end to slavery was it. Among senior commanders, Sherman's contribution to victory in that cause loomed large. In history, his stature as a "Great Captain" is secure. But that's not what the press thought, particularly in the war's early stages. In late 1861, when Sherman was commanding the Department of the Cumberland, as described in Michael Fellman's 1995 book *Citizen Sherman*, his inopportune remarks about a growing Confederate threat to Kentucky persuaded reporters that the general had either lost his nerve or gone off his rocker. "GENERAL WM. T. SHERMAN INSANE" shrieked the headline of the *Cincinnati Commercial*. The accompanying article attempt-ed to substantiate that thesis. Other newspapers embroidered and endorsed the charge: the commanding general had taken leave of his senses. The thin-skinned Sherman, who was at that time in all like-lihood suffering from clinical depression, thought his career was over and left in a funk for his home in St. Louis.

Eventually Sherman bounced back. When he did so, and as vic-tories buoyed his self-confidence, his hatred for the press knew no bounds. Throughout his life Sherman was a man of strong convic-tions that he did not hesitate to express. In his considered judgment, newspaper reporters were "toadies," "sycophants and hirelings," "sneaking, croaking scoundrels," and "damned mongrels." Newspapermen, he wrote his wife Ellen, were "the chief cause of this unhappy war. They fan the flames of local hatred and keep alive those prejudices which have forced friends into opposing hos-tile ranks." "I regard all these newspaper harpies as spies," he wrote on another occasion, "and think they should be punished as such."

He meant what he said. When, during the early stages of the Vicksburg campaign, several newspapers had the temerity to criticize his performance with phrases like "insane attack" and "insane ambi-tion," obliquely raising anew questions about Sherman's mental sta-bility, he retaliated. John Marszalek describes in his 1981 book *Sherman's Other War* how Sherman hauled Thomas W. Knox, a reporter from the *New York Herald*, before a court martial in an effort to intimidate the entire press corps accompanying his army. The charges: espionage, character assassination, and failure to obey an order (the general's own order banishing the offending reporter from his army.) Sherman's staff reminded him that he had no author-ity to try Knox or any other civilian. Undeterred, he insisted that the trial would proceed. Not only did Sherman act as the convening authority, he was also the sole witness for the prosecution, offering two days of testimony. The court duly delivered a verdict of guilty, but only on the third charge, thereby sending Sherman into a towering rage. Knox was banished. Not even a delicate intervention on the offending reporter's behalf by Abraham Lincoln, who suffered more than his fair share of journalistic abuse, could persuade Sherman to relent. From that point forward, Sherman's rule of thumb for dealing with representatives of the fourth estate remained fixed: rather than truckling in the vain hope of eliciting favorable treatment, the right approach was to "kick them and treat them as curs."

Finally, consider the case of Col. Robert R. McCormick, long-time editor and publisher of the self-described "World's Greatest Newspaper," the *Chicago Tribune*. The colonel's military title was no mere honorific. He was a veteran of World War I, a field artillery-man who had served in France as a member of the great First Division, to which he remained devoted the rest of his life. McCormick was a patriot, but that did not mean it was his business to help advance the government's policies nor to protect its national security secrets. On the contrary, when his own personal views (and therefore the *Tribune's* editorial position) diverged from those of the government, as they did with regard to the wisdom of U.S. entry into World War II, he considered it his prerogative to divulge those secrets. Thus, when in late 1941 an enterprising *Tribune* reporter in Washington secured a copy of the War Department's highly classified "Victory Plan" describing the projected expansion of the U.S. armed forces for global war, McCormick, without hesi-tation, gave the plan front-page treatment. Roosevelt's professed intent was to keep the United States out of war; he had run for an unprecedented third term on that platform. Now McCormick was ready to expose the president as a liar. On December 4, 1941, the *Tribune* offered for public scrutiny what its headlines proclaimed, not inaccurately, to be "FDR's WAR PLANS!"

Just how did the *Trib's* reporter get his hands on such a close-ly held and sensitive document? The answer in 1941 was much the same as it is today: it was leaked from the inside by a dissenter who had authorized access and sought ways to change a policy with which he disagreed. An officer assigned to the War Department had passed a copy of the plan to an anti-interventionist U.S. senator. (In 1997's *The Colonel: The Life and Legend of Robert R. McCormick,* Richard Norton Smith said the most likely source of the leak was Maj. Gen. Henry "Hap" Arnold, then commanding general of the U.S. Army Air Corps.) The senator passed it in turn to a Capitol Hill reporter employed by an anti-interventionist newspaper, with the *Tribune* effectively becoming a collaborator with elements in and out of uniform who shared a common interest in discomfiting Roosevelt.

To be sure, there have been occasions in U.S. history when civil-military-media relations operated on some principle other than antagonism expressed *against* or *through* the press. The four years beginning on December 7, 1941, have been enshrined as one such occasion. During World War II (we like to think), a cadre of senior military professionals, embodied by Gen. George C. Marshall, worked seamlessly with a chief executive-turned-master strategist to direct a successful global war effort. In fact, FDR and his military advisers often disagreed vehemently over matters of basic strategy: support for allies under Lend-Lease, the timing of the cross-channel attack, and the wisdom of the North African diversion offering only three of the most prominent examples. If World War II claims any uniqueness in this respect, it is that the military exercised notable restraint when it came to venting its dissent. Marshall himself was not a leaker.

The war tends to be remembered as a golden era in a second respect. Throughout the war (we like to think), top officials and members of the working press forged a uniformly cordial relationship based on mutual trust and understanding. In *Crusade in Europe,* Dwight D. Eisenhower recalled that in Europe it had been his policy to regard reporters "as quasi staff officers; to recognize their mission in the war and to assist them in carrying it out." One may suspect that here, as elsewhere in his ghostwritten memoir, Eisenhower was indulging in a victorious commander's understandable penchant for tidying up the battlefield. But even to the extent that Ike was accurately depicting his relations with the press, that case will remain an anomaly. As a supreme allied commander in the midst of a total war, Ike relied upon reporters exercising and enforcing among themselves extensive self-censorship. Though there were instances in which individual journalists refused to censor themselves—a famous example being Drew Pearson's revelation of the slapping incident involving Gen. George S. Patton—most complied. This is about as likely to recur in any future conflict as dropping airborne divisions behind enemy lines prior to launching a large-scale amphibious invasion.

A Fundamentally Political Relationship

Classifying relations among civilian authority, the military services, and the media as "good" (as they supposedly were in World War II) or "bad" (as in Vietnam) is an unpromising point of departure for understanding the essence of this complex, conflictive, and peculiarly intimate triangular relationship. When it comes to understanding the true nature of that relationship, the "lessons" of the past—positive in the case of Eisenhower, negative in the case of William Westmoreland—are about as relevant as are the so-called Principles of War to understanding the nature of war.

As with war itself, the essence of the civil-military-media relationship is fundamentally and inescapably political. Like war, the relationship is one of continuous and continuously shifting interaction. Unlike war, where each side exerts itself to impose its will on the other, the civil-military-media relationship combines elements of both collaboration and conflict. Ultimately, the relationship is one of dependence, based not on mutual affection or regard but expediency and self-interest. Depending on the circumstances and the interests at stake, it may involve genuine (if highly contingent) cooperation. Or it may involve exposure cloaked as disinterested "truth-telling." Or it may involve attempts, whether blatant or oblique, to manipulate or co-opt. Most likely, the relationship at any particular moment incorporates some combination of all three. It can hardly be otherwise.

When it comes to media relations, the pertinent question is never one of being "on" or "off" a team.

David Halberstam reports in his 1965 book *The Making of a Quagmire* that, having had it with skeptical Associated Press reporter Malcolm Browne at a press conference in Saigon in late 1962, Adm. Harry Felt posed a famous question to his tormentor, "Why don't you get on the team?" In doing so, he betrayed a naiveté regarding the interaction of the press with the organs of state power that was nothing short of spectacular. When it comes to media relations, the pertinent question is never one of being "on" or "off" a team. The real issue is that each participant in this trilateral relationship is pursuing an agenda, a blend of core values, institutional interests, and near-term policy objectives, salted with vanity and personal ambition. In practice, there is no unified military perspective. Within the uniformed military, interests divide according to service, command, and community. There are multiple relationships between various, often competing, military interests and a hydra-headed media. And, of course, the agenda of one side may or may not coincide with the objectives pursued by the other two sides. Where objectives happen to coincide, collaboration is in order.

Where they diverge, something other than collaboration is required.

So when it comes to civil-military-media relations, what is the question that Admiral Felt *ought* to have asked in 1962? And *to whom* should that question have been posed? As a preliminary step toward answering those questions, the balance of this paper will suggest a taxonomy of civil-military-media interaction. The purpose of doing so is not to offer up some simple formula for explaining civil-military-media relations. There is no simple formula for an irregular triangle that is in continuous flux, much like the ceaselessly careening images of a screensaver. But for present-day Adm. Felts, even a crude appreciation of some of the variants this triangle assumes just might help avoid the sort of blunders that in Vietnam laid the basis for civil-military-media dysfunction and thereby contributed mightily to American defeat.

Taxonomy of an Irregular Triangle

Interaction among civilian officials, military commanders, and the press occurs in two distinct settings. Distinguishing between the two is essential because the nature of the interaction—"the problem"—differs in each case.

The first setting involves actual operations, which may or may not include some form of hostilities. (In the aftermath of the Cold War, operations seldom rise to the level of war as such. For political reasons, the United States evinces a strong preference for classifying its frequent resort to force as something other than war.)

In these circumstances, as long as the operations appear headed for success, political and military leaders share two interests in common when it comes to relations with the media. But those interests exist in tension with one another. On the one hand, the government and the services both want to maintain the level of operational security judged appropriate to promote success in the field and to minimize casualties. Denying the enemy information that will assist him in gauging our capabilities and intentions or identifying our weaknesses and vulnerabilities is necessarily a high priority, one that points toward restraint in the release of operational details.

On the other hand, to build or sustain public support and to advance institutional interests that may relate only tangentially to the action itself, both civilian authorities and military leaders want to provide a narrative of operations as they unfold, speaking through the media to weave that narrative. Throughout the Gulf crisis of 1990-1991, for example, as part of its effort to sustain support for war against Iraq, the Bush administration offered repeated assurances that it had fully absorbed the canonical lessons of Vietnam. President George Bush was determined to dissuade Americans from viewing the war to liberate Kuwait through the lens of Vietnam. Instead, he wanted them to see it as a replay of World War II.

With this in mind, the narrative of the war that the administration offered to the media was one in which political leaders gave the field commander whatever resources he requested and then got out of the way. According to this portrayal, the objective was victory, sweet and simple, with the military permitted to fight its war without outside meddling and political restrictions. In reality, this narrative was at best an oversimplification if not an outright fabrication. Two examples of "meddling" stand out: civilian Defense Department officials rejected (Gen. Norman) Schwarzkopf's initial plan—a frontal assault—for the ground campaign and nudged him toward an alternative that emphasized maneuver. During the course of the air campaign, the administration also required him to divert assets for the famously unsuccessful "Scud hunt." But during the war itself, their war narrative served the administration's purposes well, in large part because key military figures like Colin Powell and Norman Schwarzkopf echoed the administration line—the narrative served their purposes as well—and because the media played along.

If George Bush was to some extent guilty of pulling the wool over the public's eyes, at least it can be argued that he acted on behalf of what he saw as the larger national interest. At other times, political leaders exploit military operations for purposes that are less edifying. A classic example in recent memory was Bill Clinton, in the spring of 1993, striding across the south lawn of the White House accompanied by a group of Marines just returned from Somalia. Clinton ascended to the Oval Office amidst large questions about his ability to handle foreign policy, especially as it related to the use of military power. Less than 100 days into his first term, he was already reeling from an ugly civil-military controversy, triggered by his professed intention to allow gays to serve openly in the armed forces. The carefully staged photo opportunity on the south lawn—occasioned by the hand-off of responsibility for Somalia to the United Nations—was intended to counter those impressions. With the Marines as props, it showed a confident Commander-in-Chief, fully in command of his responsibilities, comfortable in his relations with soldiers, and enjoying a first major foreign policy success. In fact, every element of that story, which the media were complicit in foisting onto the public, was fraudulent, as subsequent developments in Mogadishu would soon reveal.

Politicians are not unique in using operations for other purposes. The military itself is just as quick to do so. For example, when a particular system performs especially well—think here of the B2, viewed by many as a gold-plated hangar queen until its outstanding performance during the war over Kosovo in 1999—the services have a powerful interest in getting the word out. They do so by making their case through a frequently obliging media. It's not that the military lacks the means to communicate directly to the public;

the Pentagon's Web site (www.defenselink.mil) contains or connects to an astonishing array of information. However, messages conveyed through the prestige media carry greater weight. Whereas dozens of official Department of Defense press releases proclaiming the services' commitment to gender equality count for little, one well-placed story in the *New York Times* about female fighter pilots flying strike missions over Kosovo testifies eloquently that the services now "get it" when it comes to women.

When operations go less swimmingly, however, the civil-military dimension of the problem takes on a different aspect. No longer is the issue one of reconciling twin interests held jointly by civilian and military authorities, though in tension with one another. Rather the priority is to unload responsibility for disappointing results or outright failure, again doing so by communicating, either directly or indirectly, through the media. When things go sour, the military is especially quick to turn to the media to ensure that civilians get the blame.

Anticipating the possibility that the Gulf War could turn out badly, during the run-up to Operation Desert Storm, Gen. Colin Powell attempted to insulate himself pre-emptively from any criticism. Powell made a point of telling journalist Bob Woodward of his reluctance to use force to liberate Kuwait and his preference for continuing economic sanctions, which Woodward duly reported in his book *The Commanders.* In the event, Powell's fears proved to be unfounded, and he did not hesitate to claim his share of credit for victory.

Somalia and Kosovo provide even more vivid illustrations of this tendency. In the former case, a firefight in downtown Mogadishu in October 1993 instantly transformed the Clinton administration's first foreign policy success into an unvarnished debacle. By all rights, proximate responsibility for that failure rested squarely with the military. It was the uniformed military that had created an unworkable command structure. It was the military high command in Tampa and the Pentagon that first questioned the necessity of the reinforcements requested by the senior U.S. commander in Mogadishu. It was the overconfidence and arrogance surrounding Task Force Ranger's cavalier pursuit of Gen. Mohamed Farah Aidid that gave Somali militias their chance to turn the tables on the vastly better-equipped Americans.

The military's reflex reaction to this turn of events was to blame the civilian leaders of the Clinton administration. For its part, the administration tried to lay blame on the United Nations, always a handy target. The word out of the Pentagon faulted "mission creep," the absence of clear objectives, (United Nations Ambassador) Madeleine Albright's penchant for nation-building, and, above all, (Secretary of Defense) Les Aspin's refusal to dispatch heavy armor to Mogadishu. To an impressive degree, this campaign succeeded in deflecting attention from the military's own errors. Although no uniformed commander lost his job, Aspin lost his, with Clinton offering his head to placate an irate Congress. Meanwhile, the military transformed the firefight in Mogadishu from an unnecessary and costly failure into a gallant feat of arms, memorialized in a best-selling book and a Hollywood movie.

When operations go less swimmingly, the priority is to unload responsibility for disappointing results or outright failure, by communicating, either directly or indirectly, through the media.

In Kosovo, a similar dynamic pertained. As Gen. Wesley Clark makes abundantly clear in his recently published memoir, *Waging Modern War*, as Supreme Allied Commander, Europe (SACEUR), he shared without reservation the expectation that a demonstration of allied air power would be sufficient to persuade Slobodan

Milosevic to give way on Kosovo. If "Madeleine's War" was based on a series of illusions, the Secretary of State was not alone in embracing them.

When the bombing began, Milosevic's refusal to buckle and the surge in Serb nationalism that NATO's air campaign provoked came as an unpleasant surprise. What was supposed to have been a modest two- or three-day air campaign quickly turned into an open-ended one. Criticism of the campaign as ill-designed was instantaneous.

Within days, the Pentagon was using the press to wash its hands of responsibility for a war that was not proceeding as advertised. "Joint Chiefs Doubted Air Strategy" read the April 5, 1999 headline in *The Washington Post,* appearing while the outcome of the war was still very much in doubt. How did *Post* reporter Bradley Graham learn that the senior military leadership harbored such doubts? Through the same time-honored means the *Chicago Tribune* had employed to divine the details of FDR's Victory Plan.

Truth Lies in the Eye of the Beholder

When it comes to covering ongoing operations, the press likewise has two interests. Except where the episode is very brief (like Operation Desert Fox in Iraq) or the environment very benign (like Operation Uphold Democracy in Haiti), those interests, pursued with vigor, almost inevitably put the media at cross-purposes with responsible civilian and military authorities.

Any commitment of U.S. forces into harm's way is by definition newsworthy. To the extent that something approximating a real shooting war ensues, it is big news indeed. For a correspondent posted abroad, war has an allure equivalent to a multi-alarm fire in a downtown high-rise back home: it just doesn't get any better.

Especially for a shooting war, but even for a serious operation not involving actual hostilities—the Marines' klieg-lit landing in Mogadishu in December 1992, for example—the media attempt to do two things. First, reporters on the scene set out to tell the story itself in as much detail and with as much immediacy as their access and available technology will allow. Second, they or their editors attempt to place the story in a larger context. In all likelihood, that context will have several dimensions: human, political, diplomatic, social, environmental, and moral. What are the stakes? Who are the parties involved? What are the claims and counterclaims they advance? Whose interests are being served? Whose interests are being hurt? What are the costs and who is paying them? Most controversially, even in wartime, the media want to consider how events look from the "other side."

Those who speak for the government and the military insist that (within the constraints imposed by requirements for operational security) their intent is to provide an accurate or "true" account of what U.S. forces are actually doing. If somewhat less enamored with operational security, the media will say that that is their intent as well. Both mean what they say. But they are actually saying quite different things.

Truth, which in any armed conflict is likely to be elusive, exists to some extent in the eye of the beholder. Political and military authorities on the one hand and the media on the other come at truth, whether concerning operational details or context, from altogether different perspectives.

For the government and the military, truth emanates from the top. This is the case not simply because these institutions are organized hierarchically, but because a top-down perspective is best suited to providing a modicum of coherence to what otherwise all too easily descends into bedlam. A rectangular unit symbol on a map or video display indicates with at best partial accuracy the actual location of a company or battalion. But without that icon, posted in relation to a myriad of other icons, there would be only chaos. The "story" that political leaders wish to tell is that military action meshes seamlessly with declared political purpose. The "story" that the military wishes to tell—in some respect *needs* to tell—is the one that sustains the fiction that the generals are really in charge.

For the media, truth has multiple sources. It is as likely to come from the bottom up as from the top down, from the periphery as from the center, from the rifleman in his foxhole as from a president or commanding general presiding over a televised press conference. As the journalist and critic of journalism Peter Braestrup observed, there are "always truths to be had at battalion level." The media may not consciously set out to undermine the authority of the politicians and the generals—in truth, journalists derive gratification from their proximity to power—but the very fact that they are willing to entertain alternative sources of truth has a deeply subversive effect.

Though in the early years of the Vietnam War most correspondents readily accepted the imperative of fighting communists in Southeast Asia as part of the larger U.S. strategy of containment, the storied confrontation between sassy young correspondents like David Halberstam and Neil Sheehan and the U.S. in-country team headed by Ambassador Frederick Nolting and Gen. Paul Harkins remains the classic case. At its heart, that confrontation was an argument over truth. But the argument had two aspects. One dealt with substance. The other centered on questions of authority.

On the one hand, the reporters and the U.S. authorities in Saigon found themselves at odds because each side held radically contrary views about the reality of the Vietnam War. On the other hand, they fought one another over the question of just who had the prerogative of determining exactly what reality was.

For Ambassador Nolting and Gen. Harkins (along with Adm. Felt), truth was what they as the senior U.S. officials in Saigon declared it to be. Their preferred "story" was that progress was being made. Their preferred context was that the war was a necessary one and that if America persisted, the United States would achieve its policy objectives in the foreseeable future and at reasonable cost.

Halberstam and his fellow journalists found at least the first part to be unpersuasive. *Their* truth was discerned in the field, both witnessed directly and gleaned from conversations with U.S. advisers and others who experienced the war at first hand. Their reporting directly contradicted the official view offered by Saigon. In their judgment, the South Vietnamese government lacked legitimacy; the Diem regime was obdurate, repressive, and corrupt; ARVN (Army of the Republic of Vietnam) was inept. In essence, they implied that Saigon didn't really know what was going on; the people ostensibly in charge really weren't.

Considered in retrospect, the contemporaneous views of the reporters, contained, for example, in Halberstam's *The Making of a Quagmire* and Malcolm Browne's *The New Face of War,* stand up much better than do the optimistic pronouncements of Harkins, et al. The people in charge really *hadn't* known what was going on (or else had been guilty of wholesale dissembling and dishonesty).

Yet one can still muster a smidgen of sympathy for poor Nolting and Harkins (and their successors). The challenges of media management in a war like Vietnam were as daunting as they would prove to be protracted. There were no good choices. Attempting to muzzle the press would have been counterproductive. Limiting journalistic access, as U.S. officials would subsequently do with some success during operations Just Cause in Panama and Desert Storm in Iraq, was impractical. Meanwhile, the facts on the ground as reported by the media continued to accumulate and proved stubbornly immune to change.

Themselves unable to avoid the one thing no journalist will ever accept—namely, responsibility—the senior Americans running the war watched helplessly as their ability to shape the public's perception of reality in Vietnam gradually ebbed away. Journalists displaced high officials as the arbiters of truth. In the process, the officials found that their status, credibility, and authority were progressively attenuated. The would-be masters of events were stripped naked and held up to ridicule.

No wonder they mistook the press for the enemy.

Peacetime: The Clash of Conflicting Interests

The second setting in which civil-military-media interaction occurs is the non-operational one. Call it peacetime. Whereas interaction in operational settings tends to be episodic, apart from bizarre commitments like enforcing the no-fly zones over Iraq, we do not engage in perpetual hostilities. In peacetime, the interaction is ongoing.

Though in an operational setting the stakes can include life or death, victory or defeat, in a non-operational one, the stakes can be larger still, affecting budget share, the fate of a favored weapons system or program, or the interests of constituents crucial to winning an upcoming election. In short, while in an operational setting truth is frequently a bone of contention, when it comes to civil-military-media relations in peacetime, truth tends to figure as an afterthought, if at all. The real bone of contention is almost always politics, the clash of conflicting interests.

I noted above that when considering relations with the media, the real issue is never one of being on or off the team. (The media field their *own* team.) When it comes to understanding the realities of the day-to-day relationship of civilian to military authority, it is no less important to avoid oversimplification. In a democracy such as ours, the *principle* of civilian control forms the bedrock on which the civil-military relationship rests. But only a naïf would think that in *practice* civilian control means that responsible civilian officials call the shots the way they see them and issue orders while soldiers salute and unquestioningly obey.

The reality is a great deal messier. The civil-military relationship is a process. The central feature of that process is one of continuing negotiation. Through the interagency process, or informally, civilian leaders persuade, cajole, argue, and bargain in an effort to elicit the Pentagon's support for their policies. For its part, the military leadership (today, chiefly the Joint Chiefs of Staff (JCS)) exerts itself to shape those policies to conform to its *own* view of the nation's interests and to satisfy its own institutional requirements. When the president or the Secretary of Defense ultimately "decides," their decisions have been scripted well in advance.

This is a lesson that each new administration must learn for itself. Bill Clinton became Commander-in-Chief in 1993 thinking he was the boss. The controversy he touched off over gays in the military taught him that things were not quite that simple. Similarly, in 2001, Donald Rumsfeld became Secretary of Defense declaring he would transform the military establishment. He, too, quickly discovered that without having secured the acquiescence of the services, no transformation would occur.

The principle of civilian control obliges the military throughout this process to maintain the appearance of absolute subordination. Behind closed doors, those who represent the military's views can speak with candor. In public, the military's representatives must remain circumspect. The bully pulpit belongs to the president and remains off-limits to his generals, with rare exceptions. Douglas MacArthur thought he was one, although President Truman in 1951 demurred. Arguably, Colin Powell was a second and more recent exception. In his final year as JCS Chairman, Powell asserted and was allowed wide latitude in discussing matters of public policy. He had achieved quasi-autonomous stature. However, the need to appear subordinate often puts the military at a disadvantage, especially when the internal process of negotiation is not going its way.

To compensate for this disadvantage, the military has become adept at using alternative means to make its views known, honoring the formalities of civilian supremacy while working in practice to circumscribe it. Chief among those methods is the leak. By exposing sensitive information to public scrutiny, leakers hope to derail a policy they dislike or to introduce into the policy debate an alternative they prefer. Of course, the media outlets that receive and transmit these leaks are not entirely disinterested. By collaborating willingly (if selectively) with the military against civilian authority, they advance their own agenda.

During the course of the 1990s, an especially favored recipient of leaks relating to national security was Bill Gertz. Opponents of the defense policies of the Clinton administration found in the ace defense correspondent of the *Washington Times* a most enthusiastic partner. As a result, Gertz became famous for any number of scoops, typically based on highly sensitive documents that had come into his possession. In an appendix to his best-selling 1999 book *Betrayal*, Gertz provides a sample of the materials that came his way—almost 60 pages of documents, with security classifications ranging from confidential to top secret. The embarrassment he caused the Clinton administration was substantial.

Gertz modestly describes his own role as that of mere "conduit," passing along the concerns of individuals whom he describes as "both dissidents and patriots," even "unsung heroes." In fact, his role is much more important. Gertz and his newspaper select, amplify, embroider, and reinforce. Indeed, it is in the expectation that they will do so that the leakers offer this particular reporter and this particular paper preferred treatment.

How are we to assess the propriety of this practice, which every president in recent memory has railed against and which none has succeeded in controlling? Providing classified information to a foreign power can be treasonous. Providing the same information to Bill Gertz is (according to Gertz) an act of patriotism, even though the *Washington Times* makes the information available to any foreign power willing to drop a quarter in a newspaper vending machine. If (former CIA agent) Robert Hanssen had passed documents to an American newspaper reporter instead of to the Soviets, he would be a free man. Gertz is by no means the only recipient of such leaks. If your interest was in exposing the Clinton administration's "betrayal of U.S. military interests," he was your man. If your interest happened to be defense reform or civil-military relations, or gender, you'd take your leak elsewhere.

How does this type of military-media collaboration *against* civilian authority square with the ideal of officership?

An example of American military professionalism, Matthew B. Ridgway, wrestled with this dilemma a half-century ago. Ridgway was a soldier of exceptional courage, ability, and high moral character whose career culminated with his appointment as Chief of Staff of the U.S. Army in 1953.

As he assumed that office, the recently inaugurated Dwight D. Eisenhower was unveiling his new strategy of Massive Retaliation. In short order, Ridgway concluded that this strategy was fundamentally wrong-headed, unsustainable, immoral, and inconsistent with the military professional ethic: using vast military power not to defeat enemy armies in battle but to incinerate cities. Not incidentally, Massive Retaliation did not bode well for the interests of his own service, whose contribution to either nuclear deterrence or the conduct of all-out nuclear war would be minimal.

So Ridgway set out to overturn this policy. He tried to persuade his fellow service chiefs and the JCS Chairman Adm. Arthur Radford to join him. When it came to budget share, the Navy and especially the Air Force prospered under Massive Retaliation, so his effort failed. He requested and received a chance to present his critique of Massive Retaliation to a formal meeting of the National Security Council (NSC), with the president presiding. The NSC was unmoved. At that point Ike announced he would permit no further dissent from his military leaders. The time had come to salute and move out smartly.

Once again, the services have shown considerable skill in mobilizing media support for their effort to stymie a civilian leadership.

Ridgway remained defiant. He persuaded himself he was ethically and professionally obliged to persist in trying to reverse the administration's national security strategy, to return the United States to a military policy based on the prospect of soldiers fighting soldiers rather than of slaughtering noncombatants, a policy that would, of course, also allow a larger role for the Army. So the Army Chief of Staff proceeded to orchestrate a campaign, including targeted leaks that allowed him to enlist media outlets such as the *New York Times,* to take his case to the public. (In doing so, of course, he was necessarily revealing divisions within the U.S. military leadership over basic national security strategy to the Soviets.) The result was considerable difficulty and frustration for Eisenhower. The service in which he himself had served for more than 30 years was actively conspiring with his critics. By early 1955, the president finally concluded that he could reassert control over the Army only by sending Ridgway into retirement, which he did forthwith. (This move by Eisenhower did not succeed, however, since Ridgway's successor Maxwell D. Taylor continued to wage guerrilla war against the administration's national security policies.)

For students of the "peacetime" trilateral civil-military-media relationship, this standoff between the general and the president, in which the press (actively abetted by Ridgway) figured as a third party, retains acute salience in the present day. Today, once again, a new administration presumes to reorient basic U.S. military policy—in this case, the much-touted "transformation" to exploit the so-called "Revolution in Military Affairs" (RMA). Once again, there are many within the military, perhaps a larger and more varied group than in Ridgway's day, who view the prospect of that reorientation with considerable trepidation.

As was the case with Massive Retaliation, the RMA places at risk various service interests. The opposition to transformation from within the services is palpable to anyone who reads the newspapers. Indeed, the newspapers provide the chief outlet through which the services have vented their deep dissatisfaction with the "strategic review" process that Secretary of Defense Donald Rumsfeld initiated as a way of laying the basis for transformation. Once again, the services have shown considerable skill in mobilizing media support for their effort to stymie a civilian leadership that professes a taste for acting on its own volition. The issue is not fully decided, but the optimism with which Rumsfeld began has long since been deflated.

In the midst of this process of de facto civil-military negotiation in which the media participate as a by-no-means-disinterested third party, military officers would do well to contemplate the earlier experience of Gen. Ridgway. The situation in which Ridgway found himself engaged was far too ambiguous to permit even in retrospect a simple judgment as to whether his actions were justified or unjustified, whether Ridgway himself behaved professionally or unprofessionally.

Officers enmeshed in a comparably complicated situation today might at least consider a series of questions posed by the Ridgway case. On the substance of the matter, the wisdom and the morality of Massive Retaliation, was Ridgway right or wrong? To what degree was it his prerogative as a military officer to judge the wisdom or unwisdom of the president's policy? Were Ridgway's actions motivated (as he insisted) by honest strategic and moral concerns? Or (as his critics claimed) was it really just the fact that it was the Army's ox that was being gored? How long and by what means was Ridgway justified in opposing the president? What were the limits beyond which opposition became impermissible? What are the consequences for the nation and for the military professional ethic of pressing beyond those limits?

The relevance of these questions is by no means theoretical.

Chapter 2
How the Irregular Triangle Works

Joining Andrew Bacevich in a discussion of his paper were:

• *Gen. Dennis J. Reimer, USA (Ret.), Chief of Staff of the Army from 1995 to 1999. Gen. Reimer is currently Director of the National Memorial Institute for the Prevention of Terrorism in Oklahoma City.*

• *P.J. Crowley, former Special Assistant to the President, Deputy White House Press Secretary, and Senior Director of Public Affairs for the National Security Council. Crowley is currently Vice President of Public Affairs for the Insurance Information Institute. He also served in the Air Force 26 years.*

• *Mark Thompson, National Security Correspondent for* Time *magazine.*

H istorian Andrew Bacevich said when he began to pay attention to civil-military relations, he believed that the system of civil-military relations in this country rested on two firm pillars: the principle of civilian control and the military professional ethic.

However, during the 1990s, "a time of notable civil-military dysfunction," Bacevich concluded civilian control was something of a fiction "if by civilian control we mean that issues are identified, advice is solicited from military officers who render it to civilian authorities, and then civilian authorities make decisions and the

military salutes and executes. It is a fiction that both civilians and soldiers pay obeisance to, and it's critically important that they do that,
but it's a fiction nonetheless."

He concluded that the military professional ethic, "although
admirable in so many ways and so crucial to a sound military policy
in a democracy, also has problematic aspects." One problem is that
the professional ethic's demand for autonomy for military professionals "is a way of saying to the civilians, 'Stay out of here; you're not allowed.' That puts limits on civilian authority right there."

In reality there are three parties involved: the civilian leadership; the senior leadership of the military; and the media, particularly the "prestige media."

So Bacevich began looking for a new way to think about civil-military relations. He con-cluded that "the relationship needs to be thought of as a very loose and imperfect bar-gain that is negotiated between the services and the civilian leadership. We've had over the course of our history two or three such bar-gains that have defined civil-military relations for a particular period."

As he watched events unfold in the 1990s, Bacevich concluded
that "the bargain that had been created, probably at the beginning
of World War II and sustained throughout the Cold War, with the
great exception of the Vietnam period, had now unraveled and
would never be put together again. It unraveled under strategic
pressures, technological pressures, and perhaps most importantly,
cultural pressures. The civil-military ugliness in the 1990s was a
manifestation of the collapse of one bargain and of the inability of
soldiers and civilian leaders to negotiate a new bargain. I don't think
there is one yet; we're still struggling."

Bacevich said writing the paper made him think about the
extent to which this effort to find a new bargain is not simply a

two-party effort. In reality, he concluded, there are three parties involved: the civilian leadership; the senior leadership of the military; and the media, particularly the "prestige media."

"The media are in some instances the *medium* through which the effort to negotiate a new bargain happens, and, of course, members of the media are also participants in that they have some sense of what the terms of the bargain ought to be," he said.

The Military Point of View

Retired Army Chief of Staff, Gen. Dennis Reimer, gave observations from his experience as a senior military leader.

Reimer, who served two combat tours in Vietnam, said the concept of military-media relations in Vietnam as "a watershed event where we really got crosswise" is overplayed. During his service in Vietnam, he said, "I don't think I saw a reporter. So I didn't come away with a preconceived idea about the media."

It was not until 1989, when he became commander of Fort Carson in Colorado Springs, that he had to deal much with the media. From then on, "I was on a steep learning curve all the way until I retired in 1999," he said.

Reflecting on Bacevich's paper, Reimer said, "Civilian control over the military is intact. There are no coups being planned by the U.S. military, and every military officer in here understands he has a right and indeed a responsibility to lay out from his perspective what needs to be done. But, at the end of the day, when the Secretary of Defense says, 'This is the way we're going to do it,' you either say 'Yes, sir, I got it and I'll execute it,' or you say 'Sorry, I'm out of here.' It's that simple. I don't think there's any military officer who doesn't understand that.

"We have the responsibility to help influence events, because, ultimately, it will be military officers who take young men and women to war," he added. "And they have a responsibility to see that we do it right. So, yes, they will use every trick they can think of to make sure they get their point across, because they believe in that responsibility. And you want them to believe in that.

"Does the attitude of civilians impact on military officers' willingness to talk to the press?" Reimer asked. "Absolutely yes. You know that if you go out there and say the wrong thing, you're subject to, not necessarily adverse action, but lack of a good action."

That said, Reimer advised his military colleagues that "too many decision-makers go to work every day and figure that if the press is critical, they're losing the media war. So there is pressure to be careful about what they say. What do we do about that? For the guys in uniform, you've got to have some what I call FARs—Flat-Ass Rules. You've got to establish those and hold to them.

"You really have to establish what's going to drive you. My guiding principle was that I wouldn't talk about things in the tank. When the Joint Chiefs got together, we had what I considered very private conversations, and I did not care to pass on those conversations to anybody. I just felt that was sacrosanct. I also did not pass on direct advice we gave the National Command Authority. I don't care what those rules are, but you have to have some established, because if you start into something and don't have any, you get on a slippery slope."

Acknowledging that people in uniform will always prefer operational security over the right to know, Reimer added, "You owe it to your civilian bosses to inform them before they read about something in the *Early Bird* [a daily compendium of media stories put out by the Department of Defense]. My rule was that if I was going to go out publicly on something different from what the administration was saying, I ought to make sure that at least the Secretary of the Army knew about it, and probably the Secretary of Defense. If I didn't, I got caught short, and they had every right to hold me responsible for that."

Reimer added that it is crucial to "put the ground rules up front, whether it's on the record or off the record. Abide by those ground rules."

As for advice for the media, Reimer emphasized the importance of understanding the issues the military is dealing with and understanding better how much the military can say. With investigations, the command influence issue is always there, and commanders are not going to talk because of it, he said.

He also pointed out that military people are not going to talk about details of the Quadrennial Defense Review (QDR), "at least on the record, because the debate is still going on. Once the decision is made, they'll probably talk about it." Reimer added that at that point "they're probably going to put it in the best light they can, because they gave it their best shot and then the civilians decided this is the way we're going to do it. They're going to salute and move on out. Then the job is to execute as best you can."

Reimer challenged the media to make sure their articles are balanced, though he conceded that the military tend to consider articles balanced when they are "very favorable to us." "The military can take bad news. What we want to have is both sides of the issue presented. All the news we have out there today isn't good, so you expect your share of bad stories. But you don't expect all bad stories, continually."

An example he said the military often uses is from Bosnia, where "there are a hundred good stories, yet the one that gets reported is about the guy who raped a girl. That should have been reported; that was wrong. But what about all those other stories? Why don't they get any press? So try to be as balanced as you can."

Reimer's final challenge was to both military and media.

"Develop a relationship," he said. "The best advice I ever heard any-body give the Chairman of the Joint Chiefs was, 'do not let America wake up in a crisis and not know the Chairman of the Joint Chiefs. Get out there and get known.' It's important for the military and the media to get to know each other, so that when you face a crisis, you have some type of relationship. *Trust* is a very good word, and you have to develop it.

"There's a challenge here for both the press and the military to get the issues understood," he concluded. "These are complex issues, and there ought to be some elaboration on how things have changed, because they have changed dramatically since the Cold War. We need to spend the time to educate both the military and the press on how the issues have changed."

Reimer noted that until 1989, "we understood the sandbox we operated in; we had a strategy out there that was understood. In the Army, our job was to defeat the Soviets on the plains of Europe, plain and simple. As long as we stayed pretty close to that, we were com-fortable. We were in our lane, so to speak. But ever since the Berlin Wall went down in 1989, we have been struggling with a strategy. We've had this readiness debate, and nobody has answered the real question: readiness for what?

"Civilians are responsible for coming up with a national secu-rity strategy. The Clinton administration had a strategy based upon three pillars: to be able to respond to a crisis wherever the national security interests of the United States of America were involved and the decisions were made to put U.S. troops in place; to be able to shape the environment—make the world safer for our children and grandchildren; and to prepare for an uncertain future. If you've got something better, then somebody ought to bring it out and we ought to look at it," he said.

"Strategy is so important because it determines the force struc-ture that then gives you the basis to go in for resources," he explained.

"If you don't have that, we're just talking past each other. And I don't think we've really spent the time on this national dialogue to figure out what our national security strategy is. What is it the American people want us to do? That's what this whole debate is all about."

The Civilian Leadership Perspective

Philip J. (P.J.) Crowley, a senior spokesman during the Clinton administration, spoke from the perspective of the civilian leadership.

"With all due respect, I disagree with everything Andy Bacevich just said. The fact is that one of the reasons we're probing this relationship is expressly because the military is deferential to civilian leadership. A military does not become voluntarily 25 percent less by becoming dysfunctional and not deferential to civilian leadership.

"The bottom line is that this is just the way the founding fathers envisioned this relationship, and I suspect it's as good as it's going to get. It's also probably better than everyone in this room thinks," he said.

Citing Jeff Schaara's book *Rise to Rebellion,* he noted that the Declaration of Independence reflects the founding fathers' suspicions about both a standing army and a central government. "This tension that inherently exists in our relationship is exactly what they had in mind," Crowley said.

Referring to Bacevich's contention that politics is what fuels this relationship, Crowley said, "*Of course* it is. That's exactly right. It's not that any of the three institutions is immune to politics. In fact, the media thrive on it; civilians live by it; and the military is frequently caught in the middle, particularly when it comes to some of the budget politics."

He said the "irregular triangle" of the relationship among

military, media, and civilians in the United States is "better than it is anywhere else in the world. As dysfunctional as we might think it is, compare it with what happens in other countries. In Russia, for example, President Putin is trying to dismantle an independent media. Next door, in Ukraine, a prominent journalist has been killed, probably at the hands of the government. How high did that order go? In Nigeria, we have a resumption of civilian control of the military and of the country. This is a good thing. Fortuitously, the former military dictator had a heart attack and died. By the same token, the hero of the story is a general. How did he restore civilian control of the military? He bought off his general staff. It's nice when you're an oil-exporting country and you can do that. So, relative to these machinations in other parts of the world, we're doing just fine."

Crowley said coverage of the military has become more politicized, perhaps because fewer members of the media are covering the military. Also, a lot more news about the military is focused on Washington.

Likewise, the military is being drawn into the political dynamic. "I get a little worried when recent retirees turn around within weeks of leaving uniform and endorse a political candidate for president. That probably sends the wrong kind of message down to the troops and gets a little confusing," he said.

"Is the military clever in the ways of Washington?" Crowley asked rhetorically. "Of course it is. Does the military have a way of making sure its point of view is known? Of course it does. And by and large, at the end of the day, the system does in fact work. Is it messy? Sure. Are things distorted? Absolutely. But again, relative to how it exists in other parts of the world, it does quite well."

Noting that it is incumbent upon the civilian leadership to lead, Crowley pointed out, "It's the president of the United States who sets the agenda. Then it is for the military to provide its best counsel and advice."

Crowley worries that "we are heading for a disaster, because neither the military nor the media have yet addressed how technology has changed the battlefield. The military has lost control of the battlefield. Ten years ago, if footage needed to be taken off the battlefield, it had to be done through a military channel. Today, any of you with a cell phone and a computer have the ability to transmit information live from a battlefield without having to rely on the military. We still probably control access to the troops, but we don't control access to information. Heck, we don't even control all the intelligence sources that exist today."

He recounted his experience as a participant in a scenario exercise in which small nuclear devices exploded next to Cincinnati, Ohio. He considered it imperative that the American people be able to see what was happening at the scene, in order to ensure continuity of and confidence in government. So when he was told during the exercise that any journalist who went into the explosion area would receive a lethal dose of radiation, he demanded that the military provide the media a Predator, an unmanned reconnaissance aircraft, to be able to convey what was happening at the scene.

"This got me thinking that if I need a Predator to be able to show the American people what's happening as a crisis is unfolding, it's not a far reach to think that Jamie McIntyre and CNN/Time-Warner/AOL will at some point have the resources to have a Predator of their own," he said.

"Then what are we going to do?" he asked. "I have this great vision of Jamie with a Nintendo, working his Predator, and Craig Quigley [Deputy Assistant Secretary of Defense for Public Affairs] sitting in the next office throwing countermeasures at him to make sure we still control the imagery that's coming off the battlefield. But if we can have a Predator today that can give a live video feed from Gen. Wes Clark's office in Mons, Belgium, it's not a far step for CNN to have a Predator able to take those pictures and send them into each of our houses.

"We need to sit down and update ourselves as institutions, the military and the media," Crowley concluded. "We have to think about the implications of technology, what it has done in changing assumptions we have about control of the battlefield and how we can work together to make sure we don't have a shooting war, not between the United States and an adversary, but between the United States and the media covering our military. If institutions like the McCormick Tribune Foundation or the War College really start to work on this, we could figure out some new rules for the road."

A Voice from the Media

Mark Thompson, national security correspondent for *Time* magazine, noted that civilians don't always control the military.

"People think of the military as a monolithic block. It's not," he said. "You throw in family members and contractors and reservists, you're up to an entity the size of New York City. It's got good neighborhoods and bad neighborhoods, and gangs and chambers of commerce. Any reporter knows you work one side off the other, be it the Army against the Navy, in football or in something else, and cracks emerge that show you this is not a monolith."

Thompson cited three examples in the last administration to highlight the breakdown of the civilian-military relationship.

The first one he labeled, "Who's really in control here?" After Thompson published an article on former Secretary of Defense Les Aspin's last days in office, which ran in Aspin's hometown paper, Thompson said Aspin called and asked, "What the hell are you trying to do to me?"

Thompson said that morning, "as Les Aspin saw his professional career slipping away from him," Aspin talked about what the U.S. should do in Somalia and whether it should send the Rangers in.

According to Thompson, Aspin said, "I'm going to go with what Colin Powell tells me to do. He's the principal military advisor to the President of the United States and the Secretary of Defense. As long as Colin Powell says, 'don't send them,' I don't send them. And as soon as Colin Powell says, 'I think we ought to send them,' I send them."

"Civilian control in the military?" Thompson queried. "I don't know if Les was looking for a way out of a pickle, but the fact of the matter was, in that situation *that* Secretary of Defense felt very strongly that: (1) he had taken the advice of the top military advisor to the president of the United States, and (2) he was being hung out to dry...Les Aspin really had no role in many of those decisions, because those decisions were taken by the military, to the ultimate detriment of Les Aspin."

Thompson called his second example, "Who is telling the truth?" He said, "In all my years of covering the military, there was nothing as depressing as watching [former Chairman of the Joint Chiefs] John Shalikashvili tell us repeatedly that we were going to Bosnia for a year; that's all it would take. I talked to 14 or 16 other generals who said, 'What is he saying? We've done these gigs for years. There's no way we can do this in a year.' People just basically hunkered down. If the civilians wanted to say that we were only going to be in Bosnia for a year, one might suggest it was the military's role to say, 'Sir, you can't say that,' or 'if you say that, I'm not going to endorse it.' You could maybe argue that [former Secretary of Defense] Bill Perry had some sort of compromised position, being a civilian—an academic—and not a military man. But it was the Chairman of the Joint Chiefs who went to the Hill and assured the House Armed Services Committee and the Senate Armed Services Committee that we were going in there for 12 months, and that's all it was going to take. We're still there—what—six years later? You just would hope that your military guys would have a bit more fortitude in light of the claim of civilian control and would sometimes say, 'Gee, I just can't say that.'"

Thompson labeled his final example, from Kosovo, as "Who's Setting the Ground War Rules Here?"

"On the cusp of going into Kosovo, the White House made it known that ground troops would not be used. That essentially was an untenable position if you believed, as many people did, that air power alone might not be sufficient to drive Slobodan Milosevic out of Kosovo. Yet that was the marker that was laid down. As we crept up to day five, day 10, day 25, day 50, people began getting concerned. The air war finally cranked up; they got serious, and ultimately Slobo caved. But for a long time there was a lot of wondering in Washington about why anybody would take an arrow out of his quiver and lay it down before the battle even began. Why would you do that? That highlights the tension between military needs and political utility, and it shows that political utility will always triumph anytime there's less than a real, critical military deployment or war."

He concluded, "Each of those examples highlights for us the tension that exists between military leaders and their purported civilian leaders. The press has an important role here that sometimes we fail to carry out, in shining a spotlight, a floodlight, a magnifying glass, whatever you want to call it, on some of the equivocations made by leaders, both in and out of uniform."

Q & A: What Is Our National Defense Strategy?

Although the discussion began with typical exchanges between media and military representatives, it quickly focused on the present administration's failure to articulate a national defense strategy. A newspaper reporter asked Reimer what he would do if he were Army Chief of Staff now, with all the talk of cutting back two Army divisions.

"Would you talk on background with the press about how these guys are out to lunch? Would you say to the press, 'These folks are increasing the risks to soldiers?' And if you would, at what point would you stop? When the Secretary of Defense makes a final decision on his strategy and QDR? Or would you continue after that point and take it to the Hill? And what if Rumsfeld said to all the chiefs, 'I know you guys might be upset with what I plan on doing, but I don't want you to talk to any reporters or anybody else about this.'"

Noting that he doesn't know that cutting back two divisions has been put on the table, Reimer said, "If they believe that would be ill-advised, and I certainly believe it would be ill-advised, they've got to make that point. They have every legitimate right to make it in any way they can as long as this discussion's going on and no decisions are made. The Army has to tell their story. How they do it is kind of up to them, and they've done a fairly good job on that particular subject."

However, he continued, "Why are we arguing whether you've got too many Army divisions or whether you've got too many ships, when we haven't got the front-end piece right? What is the strategy? What do you want us to do? That's where I would make my push to say, 'Look, tell us what you want the military to do, and then let us construct the military.'

"But you can't do that overnight, so this whole thing about change and transforming the force is no more than an academic exercise. A lot of people have great ideas, but the people who are going to fight are the ones wearing the uniform. And if you don't like what they're doing, then you ought to get rid of them and get a new group.

"And if the Secretary said, 'I don't want you talking to the press,' that's a point where you make one of those decisions about whether you can live with that or whether you go out and do something else," he concluded.

Another conferee pointed out that civilian leadership includes not only the executive but also the legislative branch. Crowley agreed: "The civilian leadership in Congress has a role to play. They ultimately control the purse strings. They're a factor that has to be weighed in."

Noting that the need to work with Congress puts pressure on the executive branch to present a unified point of view, he pointed out that the military have their own means of communicating with Congress: the annual "wish list" prepared by the services.

"Every commander, rightfully, is saying, 'I need this. I need this. I need this,'" Crowley said. "I've never met a military leader who said, 'I've got enough. Don't give me any more.' But someone's got to draw the line, and that line is drawn by the Congress."

However, he concluded, "it's another area that reaffirms that, ultimately, the military will defer both to the executive branch in terms of priorities and to the Congress in terms of the amount of money it gets to spend. It's an ugly system, but it does work."

The discussion heated up when a radio journalist said that in many years of covering the Pentagon, "I have never seen what is almost tantamount to open revolt on the part of the military against the civilian leadership. I have two- and three- and four-star officers coming to me, and I know I'm not alone in this, not only bad-mouthing the current civilian leadership such as I've never heard before, but talking about things that are really rather frightening, about the results of certain things if the civilian leadership was able to carry them out."

A general responded: "I've been involved in the QDR process now for two years, and when the new administration came in and took us on a different course, all the work we'd done jointly with the joint staff was shelved. We were pushed aside, as these very secretive study groups came to be and worked in isolation. But if that was the way the Secretary [of Defense] wanted to do it, that's fine. Certainly he wanted to get separate opinions before he brought the military in; we understood that.

"I don't think there's dissension with the Secretary," the general added. "He's got a group of trusted agents who are trying to work things for him. They may have his guidance, and they may be operating on broad guidance or intent. The issues coming out of the QDR largely revolve around this small circle of advisors who really don't embrace the notion that senior military officials might know what they're doing. The rub is not with the Secretary; it's with those who have been entrusted to run these various processes for him."

The general went on, "Until the Secretary or the Deputy come to some conclusion, you're going to have constant tension between those subordinates who are running some pretty wild notions around the Pentagon, as well as multiple leaks. We've got to come to a conclusion on this thing—at least get something down, start debating and discussing it, get a decision, and then move out on it."

Contrasting the last QDR with the current one, the general said, "That was clearly a fiscally driven exercise. We knew it from the start, so we set out on a course to figure out how to gain an additional $15 billion for procurement. In all my years in the service, I've never seen anything like this. But I don't think it's open revolt. I think we don't have the decisions we need. The course is not clear, and we have some people empowered to run the issues on some very curious azimuths that have created a lot of tension within the services."

A print reporter demurred: "This QDR process is very gentlemanly compared to '97 and '96, when the services were at each other's throats, especially the Army and the Air Force, over who won the Gulf War and how those lessons should fold into the next QDR. That reflects some of the civilian leadership and the military leadership over the last year saying, 'We're going to have a more civil debate.'"

A newspaper reporter expressed strong concern over proposed legislation to allow criminal prosecution of anyone leaking classified information.

Moderator Jeff Smith noted that under current law, it is illegal for someone to leak a classified document if they know its release could harm national security. The proposed revision would make it a criminal act to release any "properly classified" information. There would be no requirement for the government to prove that releasing the information could be harmful; the mere fact of using classified information could lead to criminal prosecution.

He also pointed out that "leaks have traditionally been part of the democratic process, and though leaks can be damaging, at the same time, government employees can abuse the classification system to hide malfeasance or embarrassing incompetence."

He said media representatives have an obligation to check with government officials prior to publication to determine, for instance, if publication or broadcast would harm national security.

A senior Marine Corps officer observed that existing laws should be sufficient to prosecute improper release of classified information appropriately.

The reporter asked, "Does the potential for leaks influence policy planning?"

A senior Air Force officer responded, "There's a certain frustration when leaks cause inside, 'family' matters to be made public. But in the final evaluation, what difference does it make to the final outcome? Most often, none."

Bacevich saw parallels between the present situation and the controversy surrounding gays in the military: "The Clinton administration in 1993 and this administration this year were alike in the sense that a newly elected civilian leadership came into office and said, 'We know what needs to be done.' They were going to announce a decision, and everybody was going to sign up to do it. And both administrations learned that's not the way the game is played. Both were severely punished. And the media are the medium through which the punishment is exercised in order to bring the civilian leadership to a proper understanding of the need to negotiate rather than simply direct."

Another print journalist said, "Having just chronicled the Clinton administration, I can say that clearly there were a lot of ill feelings toward the Commander-in-Chief. In Bosnia in particular, from colonels to sergeants, it wasn't open contempt, but it was fairly contemptuous, with people describing him as a draft dodger. But the big thing was, when Clinton came to visit Bosnia, they had to disarm all the MPs [military police]. That left a lot of MPs standing around with assault rifles with no clips in them, and that spoke volumes. It was unprecedented. They were afraid somebody was going to take a shot at the Commander-in-Chief."

Crowley interjected, "The Secret Service determines who is going to be responsible for what role in protecting the president of the United States. I would challenge not your facts, but your conclusions based on those facts."

Smith added, "It's conceivable that the GIs who did not know that was standard procedure drew the conclusion that the military leadership or the Secret Service was afraid they were going to shoot the president. Whereas, in fact, it's simple standard procedure done perhaps anyway."

Crowley said he would not necessarily characterize either the situation of 1993 or the current situation as confrontations between the civilian leadership and the military. "They are actually confusion and confrontations between civilian and civilian, with the military in the middle," he said.

"In 1993, what fueled the gays in the military issue was in part an unfortunate circumstance, with a high-profile Navy case being tried in the press at the same time a presidential candidate made a statement on his beliefs. It became an early contest between the Clinton administration and partisans on the Hill. Absent that kind of political fuel, it was much more likely that this would have been an issue that would have been resolved much more quietly, and certainly not the first one out of the box. This is not what a new administration wanted to confront as it walked through the door.

A candidate said, 'Help is on the way.' And then all of a sudden, there's not the same kind of money available.

"Likewise, this year, the confusion is within the administration itself," Crowley added. "A candidate said, 'Help is on the way.' And then, with both his policy of tax cuts and the economic impact of the downturn, all of a sudden, there's not the same kind of money available. The military is just trying to figure it out: 'Hey, we thought we heard you a certain way, now we have a different set of criteria.'

"In both cases it was not a confrontation between these two institutions, but just the politics of both occasions that sometimes takes the system haywire until they finally sort it out politically," he said. "It's going to take some time to work this thing out. But by the same token, the chief executive said, 'We're going to review a whole lot of things,' and the military said, 'Yep, we'll do it.' So I don't see this necessarily in the same light as others."

Smith noted that he was chief of the transition team for Clinton at the Pentagon in 1992 and 1993 and was responsible for all issues in defense except gays in the military, which was done by a separate group that kept him informed.

"I was appalled on the Wednesday evening before the inauguration to get a memorandum to the president, with an executive order attached [regarding gays in the military], and immediately sent a memo to Les Aspin," he recalled. "He was equally appalled."

Smith said he and another advisor quickly drafted a memo from Aspin to the president-elect saying, "This is a terrible thing. Whatever you do, don't sign this. Put in place some kind of process to look at it; it's a serious issue. You've made a pledge, but don't sign this executive order as the first thing you do."

"That was on Friday," Smith said. "Les Aspin went on, I think, *Meet the Press* on Sunday morning before the inauguration. Someone leaked all three memos: my memo to Aspin, the memo Aspin and I did to the president-elect, and the underlying memo with the draft executive order. That all appeared in the *New York Times* that Sunday morning.

"Now, somebody used the press to put the president-elect in a position that he and his people felt they couldn't back down from," he said. "I have no idea who did that. But it's an example of how the press was used. Yet it was a very legitimate news story, and it was handled, in my judgment, professionally by the press. To the extent mistakes were made, they were made by the incoming administration in not dealing with the situation terribly well. But it's an example of how a well-placed leak painted various parties into corners, and the chance of some more negotiated, thoughtful response did not have the occasion to play out."

A television correspondent drew his own parallel between 1993 and the current situation: "In 1993, President Clinton alienated some of the military by attempting to fulfill a campaign promise to allow homosexuals to serve in the military. In the current situation, President Bush has alienated some of the military by failing to follow through on his campaign promise that 'help is on the way.'"

"Both Rumsfeld and Aspin were saddled with no-win situations based on promises and statements made by a president," he pointed out. "Aspin had to deal with the homosexual policy, which was a no-win, and Rumsfeld now has been saddled with this perception that he was going to do a top-to-bottom, thorough review and radically reform the Pentagon, something that's turned out to be a sort of no-win proposition for him.

"The other striking difference," he said, "is that the Clinton administration, although they made cuts in that first year when everyone agreed the Cold War was over and we were talking about a peace dividend, turned out to be very deferential to the military and, in fact, funded almost all the programs that the military wanted. Of course [George W.] Bush is in the opposite situation in *not* being very deferential to the military and having alienated some of them."

A newspaperman wondered if there had been any surveys charting interest outside Washington in the various disputes within the Pentagon. Noting that "we focus on these things because we are reporters in Washington," he questioned the utility of reporting on these "squabbles" until an actual decision has been made. He suggested that doing so might, perhaps, "fuel this notion that we're only interested in reporting controversy and personality clashes, and in the end perhaps what's really important is the ultimate product of this process that's going on."

"That's a very valid point," Reimer said. "In Oklahoma, there's a whole lot more interest in the Sooners than there is in what's happening in the QDR. I would also say that what happens in the QDR is much more significant. But the American people, unless it's a crisis, are occupied like the people in Oklahoma. They're into football, or the price of wheat, or the issues that affect them.

"You all have an important job," he stressed, "to keep this argument at the right plane, because this is critical. If we do it wrong, 20 years from now we'll pay the price. That's why the military believes so strongly in what they're doing right now. This is not an academic exercise, where we lose a football game. We're going to lose troops, and that's bad."

An admiral agreed: "During the summer, I went back to my hometown in rural Iowa and we aren't on their scope. It is not a part of their world. They do not feel threatened by any nation or outside agency. They care about issues that are much more relevant to their day-in/day-out lives."

He added, "I'm not at all sure that you're not just seeing here an awful lot of light and smoke and heat being put on an issue that a lot of people feel very passionately about. That's healthy. We ought to be arguing and fighting at this point in this process.

"There are a lot of ideas being floated right now," the admiral said. "A lot of people think this is really, really important. There is a sense that this is an inflection point in America's military as we move forward into the 21st century, and we've got to get it right. Not surprisingly, you have some people with very strong feelings on all sides of the issue."

A former Pentagon official added, "The exception to general public indifference is base closure. If you have a base in your area, *everybody* cares. Base closure also raises an interesting example of the shifting triangle, because at some point, for example, it's the Army against the Air Force on an issue. At some point, it's the Third Armored Division against the Third Infantry Division. And how does that play inside the military? How do the military officers at these bases deal with their communities in competing perhaps against other members of their own service for continuation of mission?"

A newspaper reporter pointed out that, regardless of the apparent lack of interest by ordinary Americans in struggles between the military and civilian leadership, "I don't think we can wait until the end of September to suddenly announce: 'These are the plans of the great Defense Secretary.' A big part of this story is the criticism from the officers in all the services. They are shaping and molding this process. It's our responsibility to cover this. We might not write about it every single day, but this is clearly a running story, and it's important for us to birddog it."

Crowley replied, "Whether the American people are attentive at any particular time is not necessarily relevant to the process we are talking about here. What happens every Tuesday and Thursday at the Pentagon, or every day at the White House, or every day at the State Department is vitally important to put on the record so the information is available to the American people, because at some point in time somebody out there is paying attention. My in-laws in Boston watch C-SPAN all the time. I'm sure there's a fairly healthy audience there, so the fact that we continue to have this conversation even though the American people may be listening with one ear is vitally important to what we do."

He also noted that transitions take time. "Statistics show it used to take a few months. Now it is well over a year before the president, any president, has his advisors in place to where he can actually move out. A transition means that a president and his team are learning on the job. That happened in 1993; it's happening now. It's painful, and it's by no means a straight line," he said.

"I would caution you that ultimately administrations *do* learn," Crowley said. "Certainly, with the Clinton administration, you had a relationship that probably could not have started more badly. You had a group of incoming civilians and a military establishment that had less in common than any similar team in our history, and yet, over eight years, both sides worked very hard to develop a functional relationship where both sides did, each in its own way, what the American people needed them to do."

He continued, "You can report the warts as they exist, and they certainly do, and the mistakes that are made, and they're certainly made, but I would caution you that you probably should be prepared to give the incoming team credit that they have learned something as they have gone through this very difficult process."

As a final point, Crowley said that, for the most part, the media's perception of the relationship between Clinton and the military did not change over time: "There was never a story about the Clinton administration and the military that didn't include Clinton's problem with the military. I always reacted badly to that because that actually does a disservice to the military as much as it does a disservice to the president. The president had no trouble with the military, because the military was going to salute and ultimately do what he wanted, whether they voted for him, liked him, or not. That is the essence of what this relationship is, whether we like everything a chief executive says or his minions say, ultimately the military as an institution is going to salute that chief executive and follow his lead. So this system does work."

An Army general recalled that though the Clinton-military relationship was strained at the beginning of his term, and though he "was not the role model we would have chosen, we both learned to respect each other. Clinton learned that the military is organized to get something done. The military learned that nobody could focus on an issue like Clinton could."

Chapter 3
Challenges and Opportunities

The next panel's purpose was to assess the new Bush administration's challenges and opportunities regarding dissemination of national security information, its attitudes and performance to date, and key issues on its horizons. Representatives of the Bush administration were invited but did not attend. However, two conferees who served in the previous administration of President Clinton gave insight into the perspective of civilian leadership in general. Panelists were:

• CNN Pentagon Correspondent Jamie McIntyre;

• Bloomberg News Pentagon Correspondent Tony Capaccio;

• Rear Adm. Craig Quigley, Assistant Secretary of Defense for Public Affairs;

• Maj. Gen. Kevin Byrnes, the Army's Deputy Chief of Staff for Programs;

• P.J. Crowley, Special Assistant to the President and Deputy White House Press Secretary in the Clinton Administration, who is now Vice President of the Insurance Information Institute;

• Jeffrey Smith, Partner in the Washington law firm of Arnold & Porter, who has held many executive and legislative branch positions, including service as General Counsel for the Senate Armed Services Committee and for the Central Intelligence Agency and as Chief of President Clinton's transition team at the Department of Defense.

C NN Pentagon correspondent Jamie McIntyre said that both during and after the campaign, the Bush team was very effective in portraying themselves as the pro-military choice. He recalled the day before the election, when, to thunderous applause at a campaign rally in Grand Rapids, Mich., Bush announced that he had a message for all the men and women in uniform, their parents, and their families: "Help is on the way." McIntyre said Bush used a series of speeches during the campaign to criticize the Clinton administration's handling of the military, describe the military as being in a decline and assert that his administration would reverse that decline. The speech that struck him most was Gen. Norman Schwarzkopf's address to the Republican convention, in which he criticized the Clinton administration, saying that as of 1999, the number of Army divisions ready for war had shrunk to less than half of what they had been before Desert Storm.

"Of course, what was left out was the fact that most of those cuts had come under Defense Secretary Cheney [in the first Bush administration]," he pointed out. "Some argument might be made that the real problem comes with the final cuts, not the beginning cuts, but those remaining cuts were overseen by Colin Powell and Les Aspin when there was a broad consensus back in the early 1990s that the Cold War was over and there should be a peace dividend of some sort. That notion went away pretty quickly, but back there in the heady days of 1993, it did seem like there might actually be a peace dividend to be reaped."

Noting that Bush continued to focus on the military as the election drew nearer, McIntyre said, "We'll never know the effect that the military vote had on the election, but we know that the absentee votes were crucial in Florida, and we know that the military vote did split in favor of George W. Bush."

Not surprisingly, many in the military anticipated great things from the new, apparently pro-military Bush administration.

"I remember having some very spirited discussions with a young, enthusiastic Marine captain," McIntyre said. "All during the last year of the Clinton administration, he had come into my office with various charts and graphs showing the shortage of spare parts, the decline in resources they were suffering in the Marine Corps; telling me how awful the Clinton administration had been and how much he was anticipating things being better under George W. Bush. I remember warning him not to automatically assume that would be the case. Playing the devil's advocate, I argued with him about whether we'd actually see any significant increase in defense spending, particularly beyond what a Gore administration might have been forced to spend because of political reasons."

> "I didn't find a whole lot of difference, with the exception of the issue of gays in the military. Nevertheless, Bush was very effective in portraying his stand as more favorable to the military."

He also remembered debates during the campaign with his editors, who wanted him to write stories about how different the Bush and Gore defense positions were. McIntyre said, "I didn't find a whole lot of difference, with the exception of the issue of gays in the military. But on missile defense, on defense spending, on rebuilding the military, they were both saying very similar things. Nevertheless, Bush was very effective in portraying his stand as more favorable to the military."

Once Bush was in office, he appointed Donald Rumsfeld as Secretary of Defense. However, McIntyre observed that though Rumsfeld "was not part of the team that helped put together the campaign and write some of those speeches Bush gave, he was given the task of conducting this top-to-bottom review. The first problem, of course, is this perception that this is going to be a comprehensive overhaul that's going to result in a real shake-up at the Pentagon. Privately, Rumsfeld started downplaying those expectations, saying he was not a radical reformer, that he was going to be looking at things very carefully, that it's not easy to change a big institution. But the expectations were building publicly, in large part because of things the president was saying in public. At each appearance, he would mention that he had asked Rumsfeld to conduct what he called a comprehensive review that was going to radically change how the Pentagon met the threats of the 21st century. So Rumsfeld was saddled with this perception right away that he was doing a very comprehensive review, even though he kept saying privately that wasn't exactly what was going on."

For instance, McIntyre said, "In an interview with CNN in May, when Wolf Blitzer asked him about this top-to-bottom strategic review, Rumsfeld said, 'First of all, it's not a top-to-bottom review. It's quick and dirty studies, where we're looking at key priority areas.' In briefings, people would ask, 'Where did this perception come from, that you were doing a comprehensive review?' And Rumsfeld kept saying, 'Well, I was never the one that gave that impression.'

"Of course, while he's saying publicly, 'I'm just figuring things out. I've asked a lot of smart people to help me. You guys are expecting too much right away,' behind the scenes there's all kinds of machinations going on, which seem to indicate that there are radical reforms in the works," McIntyre added.

"The first thing that really gets everybody stirred up is the appointment of Andy Marshall to do a paper on strategy review," he said. "When Tom Ricks first reports on this in *The Washington Post* on Feb. 9, he's got a big headline that says, 'Pentagon Study May Bring Big Shake-up; Unconventional Defense Thinker Conducting Review.' Ricks, familiar with Andy Marshall and his views about questioning aircraft carriers, heavy armor, and conventional ways of thinking, has put two and two together here: Marshall is heading the review and he's a radical thinker—therefore, there's going to be radical reform.

"Of course, no sooner does this story come out than the Pentagon starts downplaying it," McIntyre said. "Marshall's not in charge of the review, they say. Rumsfeld's in charge of the review; Marshall's just doing a paper. He's going to turn it in to the Secretary. It's not the big strategy. But the stories continue to roll. Once that theme gets out, people latch onto it. The *Christian Science Monitor* does another piece: 'Pentagon Braces for a Makeover.' The following week: 'Bush assigned big-picture review of the military to an iconoclastic analyst who may file report this week.' And the fury starts going.

"Meanwhile, at the Pentagon we're beginning to hear discontent from the services, who are feeling cut out of the process," he said. "They don't have access to these review panels. They're not being told what's going on. When they do meet with Rumsfeld, they're able to talk to him, but they don't get any sort of feedback about where things are going. And the perception starts to slide. In the meantime, we're all looking for these big changes that might be coming down the path, and they don't seem to be happening.

"One big question is, what's happening with the two-war capability?" McIntyre said. "Again, *The Washington Post* is out in front on this story, reporting on May 7 in Tom Ricks' front-page story, 'Defense Secretary Donald H. Rumsfeld set to unveil sweeping changes in U.S. military strategy, including the formal abandonment of the two-major-war yardstick that for a decade has been used to determine the size of the military.'

"Again, the story comes out and everyone starts downplaying it," he said. "Rumsfeld says he hasn't decided on anything. They want to replace the two-war strategy, but they're not going to do it until they have something better, and he's not sure what they have is better.

"Again, we're getting this discordant message between what Rumsfeld is saying publicly, and what we're hearing privately, and what Steve Cambone [Principal Deputy Under Secretary of Defense for Policy] is telling people, and the marching orders that are being given to different groups," McIntyre said. "The message is becoming so muddled that almost every time we run into Rumsfeld we're trying to get him to explain what's actually going on. And Rumsfeld keeps harking back to the same phrase, 'Change is hard; it's going to take a while. There's a work in progress. We haven't made any decisions. We're just thinking about these things. We're asking all the right questions. We're going to do the right thing in the end.' But now it's six months down the road."

McIntyre said the first six months have been "marked by a lot of difficulty figuring out what they want to do. There's no clear message coming from the Pentagon. What seems clear one day, the next day changes."

Tony Capaccio, Pentagon correspondent for Bloomberg News, put himself in the role of good cop in assessing the Bush administration's first six months: "Compared to 1993, and all the trauma Aspin and the American public went through with gays in the military, women in combat, Haiti, and the failed raid in Somalia, this year is a taffy pull. This is not earth-shaking if you take the long view of prior administrations. Saying that, however, the bar was a lot higher for this group coming in.

"Part of the reason expectations have not been muted is that Rumsfeld didn't have his team in place, and the message ran past him," he said. "He talked off the record, but there wasn't any attempt, really until mid- to late-May, to start muting expectations of these sweeping reviews."

He said the tone was set with a Sept. 23, 1999, speech at the

Citadel, in which President Bush said, "Even if I'm elected, I will not command the new military we create. That will be left to a president who will come after me. The results of our effort will not be seen for many years."

"Right there, transformation is a process; it's not a document," Capaccio said. "That's what they're saying now, but he said it two years ago, and they need to keep on top of that as a message. Instead, they let these stories come out from analysts and unnamed sources of 'sweeping this' and 'sweeping that.'

"One of the challenges they face in the next six months is to put in English what they are doing and how that differs from Clinton's policy of engagement," he said. "But these are not fatal flaws; it's not that they can't rebound. Gen. Reimer made the point that the Clinton administration's relationships with the military matured from 1993 on, after a rocky, terrible first year. This administration certainly has not stumbled to the point where they've broken an ankle and have to be put to pasture."

He added that there is a perception in the analyst community that "maybe Rumsfeld's too out of touch for what the U.S. needs by way of vigorous new strategy. We all have to remember he was not the first choice. He was not one of the Vulcans who crafted the Citadel speech. He was a second choice, maybe even a third choice."

Capaccio said the administration's handling of the supplemental appropriations bill was its first mistake: "That showed the administration didn't have it together in terms of a defense budget plan."

He recalled how Bush had told a group of GOP leaders that "good appropriations have to follow a good review. That was a front-page story in the *New York Times* because it framed for a lot of readers and Republicans that this guy's not a pushover. There's going to be a review, unlike what [former Secretary of Defense] Cap Weinberger got away with when Reagan first came into office in 1981. He got a $32 billion add-on to the 1981 and 1982 budgets without any strategic review; it was pigs at the trough."

Though Capaccio said the Bush administration deserves some credit for suggesting a review was in progress, this positive point was negated when, four days after Bush's speech, "they came out with a notice from the National Security Council: no supplemental [appropriations request] in 2001. That got the administration involved in a firefight they didn't need early on. While they were trying to craft a defense plan, while they were trying to translate the rhetoric of the campaign into something tangible, they angered a lot of Republicans. To the glee of a lot of Democrats, they seemed to be self-destructing. They had to pull back, and the supplemental came out a couple months later."

According to Capaccio, this was a clear indication that the tax cut and economic issues took precedence over military issues for the administration. "Though rhetoric about the military was there during the campaign, they were really fixated on the tax cut early on, and didn't want that message to be derailed," he said. But as a result of the tax cut and economic downturn, once-rosy surplus projections have dwindled into dust. The result, said Capaccio, is that Rumsfeld is "locked into a corner."

One of the big challenges for the administration is to delineate clearly what threats the U.S. faces, why this new strategy fits and how it can be accomplished with fewer dollars, he said. "Rumsfeld and the Pentagon keep blindly ignoring that issue when you ask them about it."

He added that Republicans and Democrats alike were "stunned that Rumsfeld did not try to take on the Office of Management and Budget earlier this year when he submitted a $40 billion package for 2002 and it came back as $18.5 billion. Rumsfeld should have at least communicated privately through leaks or background that he was upset with this. He's played too good a soldier here if he's going to try to mobilize public support, because right now this is seen as an inside-the-beltway battle."

Capaccio also said he thinks the Bush administration "made a fatal and stupid mistake early on by lumping together tactical and strategic missile defense. They lumped together systems that aren't going to be around for maybe seven or eight years with those to protect soldiers in the field.

"It's not at all clear that's going to result in a military that's substantially different from what we had or is in any way less capable of fighting the two wars than today's military."

"If you just frame the debate as a missile defense system, you lose the fact that the first systems in the Bush plan are going to be a tactical missile defense. They've got to explain to the public that they're going to first protect their sons and daughters, not worry about a North Korean missile defense threat; that's way down the line. Most of the public, I submit, would agree that those are valid priorities, but when you package the program as a missile defense umbrella with no differentiating, you're going to get in a lot of trouble and you're going to lose the debate," Capaccio said.

The other issue with missile defense is dollars, he said. "Eight billion dollars of an $18.5-billion package is a lot, no question. But the Democrats were going to submit, if they won, about a $5.3-billion missile defense program, so it's a $3-billion increase. That's a lot of money, but most of the money goes for increased testing. A challenge ahead for the administration is to explain clearly what this money is going for."

McIntyre interjected that, as an observer at the Pentagon, "I have to give the Bush administration credit for one thing: taking credit for things that were already going to happen. A good example of this is the 4.6 percent increase in pay for 2002 that President Bush announced for U.S. troops. He told the troops, 'You know, our budget includes the money for this pay raise.' Of course, the amount of that pay raise was mandated by Congress; it's set by a formula. Had President Bush done absolutely nothing, the troops would have gotten a 4.6 percent pay raise."

McIntyre pointed out that the Bush administration is also portraying nuclear arms reductions as a new initiative—again, something that was happening already. He observed that as part of the START (Strategic Arms Reduction Treaty) negotiations, the United States was already committed to reducing the number of warheads to 3,500. And the United States already had committed in principle to go immediately to START III negotiations, which would have cut the number to 2,500.

"We don't know what the number will be in the Bush administration, but it's likely to be around 2,000 or 2,500, and we're already on that track. Now, Bush eventually indicated that he might do this unilaterally, which would be a change, but we haven't actually done that; we're still in discussions," he said.

McIntyre concluded, "There have been several cases where they have portrayed things that were already in the works as Bush administration initiatives. At the same time, they've really failed miserably in explaining what's going on with the two-war capability and what's replacing it. We have a pretty clear idea that they want to get rid of the two-war capability as a force-sizing mechanism, but it's very unclear still what they're replacing it with, even though Rumsfeld keeps explaining it to us.

"It's not at all clear that's going to result in a military that's substantially different from what we had or is in any way less capable of fighting the two wars than today's military, recognizing, of course, that this two-war capability has always been a myth. We never had the two-war capability, and Rumsfeld admitted as much recently," he said.

Capaccio said the Bush administration "really has been disingenuous" regarding the military budget. He noted that the Clinton administration was planning a $310 billion military budget. The Bush administration added $14.5 billion late last year. Capaccio said, "[White House spokesman] Ari Fleischer and the White House staff kept insisting, 'No, 310's our budget number, 310's our budget number; 296 is the base.' Three ten is what Clinton left. The administration should be given credit for getting $18.4 billion, because the cumulative effect is the largest defense increase since 1982-ish— about 7 percent in terms of real growth. Give them credit for that, but they kept trying to take credit for this 310 figure."

A Military Assessment

Rear Adm. Craig Quigley, Assistant Secretary of Defense for Public Affairs, began the military assessment by characterizing Secretary of Defense Donald Rumsfeld as "a very cautious and deliberate man. He keeps his thoughts to himself and to a small group of people he has known for many years and has come to trust. He does not give trust easily or quickly to those whom he has only recently met. And he has a tendency to rely on the advice of that group of people he has known for many years.

"He is conservative," Quigley said. "By that I don't necessarily mean only his political views. For example, as he has said often of the 2-MRC [Major Regional Conflict] capability: 'I am not going to take something away or deconstruct something until and unless I have a better idea waiting in the wings that I can put in to take its place.' Only recently has he come up with what he considers a better idea."

He noted that the "abandonment of the two-major-war yardstick" is what Rumsfeld "thinks is the better way to go. That is, to have the ability to go in and completely conquer a country, take over its capital, and change the regime."

In addition, Quigley said, "Simultaneously, you would have the ability to fight an enemy in another part of the world to a standstill and to blunt an enemy's advance, to stop an invasion. I would use Korea as a historical example, perhaps. And, simultaneously with both of those, we would continue to do peacekeeping things such as we see today in Bosnia, Kosovo, and elsewhere around the world. That is where his thinking is evolving."

Turning to missile defense, he pointed out that "62 percent of Americans think we have a missile defense system now, and that's flat wrong. We have a great ability through U.S. space command to watch missiles come in, and you can predict when and where they're going to hit, but that's all. And when you tell people that, they are somewhat shocked.

"I do not agree with Tony that it was a mistake to aggregate missile defense capability," Quigley added. "You notice that it's not called National Missile Defense anymore. That is intentional. It is meant to protect the United States, our troops and friends overseas, and it will be both tactical and strategic in nature." Noting that the administration is attempting to "tell people very clearly this isn't Ronald Reagan's strategic defense initiative," he added, "We don't know what it's going to look like. We know that we're going to do a heck of a lot of testing, and we will continue to pursue the systems that seem to work well and stop the ones that don't. It just seems to make sense.

"The perception vs. reality cliché is very real," Quigley said. "In the past several months there has been one eruption after another of the theory of the day about how many divisions, how many carrier battle groups, how many fighter squadrons we're going to cut. This is a reflection of the Secretary's effort to try to ask hard questions and come up with a clear, coherent defense of why we have what we have. And if you can't give a good, clear, coherent defense of why we have what we have, he will question the validity of the notion in the first place.

"Now, that scares a lot of people, because it gores a lot of oxes and a lot of long-held, bedrock beliefs in the utility of some systems and some units," Quigley said, adding that this does not imply that Rumsfeld is necessarily opposed to nor wanting to cut them. "He just challenges the conventional wisdom and forces the system to have a very clear, thought-through argument of why we need what it is we say we need," he pointed out.

"Do not underestimate the impact of the change that has already been put in place," Quigley warned. "People have a tendency to want to count *things*: how many units, how many ships, how many planes. Some significant things that have already been put in place will make a difference. Never before, in my knowledge, has there been an administration with such an extensive business background. They're going to take a real green eyeshade sort of look at the way the military departments do business, and there will be some significant changes based on their deliberations."

Noting that at the beginning of President Bush's term "there was some perception that there was going to be radical change in a couple of months," Quigley asserted, "That's just not Don Rumsfeld's style. For those who had that expectation, it isn't about to happen."

The next speaker was Gen. Kevin Byrnes, the Pentagon's Deputy Chief of Staff for Programs. Moderator Jeff Smith asked Byrnes, "You are in one of the forward trenches on the QDR. Is it true that there is a difference between perception and reality?"

"Yes," said Byrnes. "Part of the service perspective we bring to this QDR comes from the last effort, which tore the services apart and put them at one another. There were a lot of internal service-to-service contests, and within the services among their components——the active guard, the reserves—a lot of infighting.

"So we set out to do a lot better in this QDR," Byrnes said, "particularly to hold together the teams internal to our components as well as the services. One of the great points of this QDR that we take for granted is that you don't see services *at* one another. It's a non-story right now because we believe in joint war fighting. The QDR will strengthen our ability to do that.

"From an Army perspective, and from a service perspective overall, what we hoped to get accomplished more than anything else in this QDR was a recognition of the strategy," he said, "to structure, to resource any mismatch that existed and how we were going to come to grips with that.

"First," Byrnes said, "was to recognize the condition of the current force and where it is in terms of its readiness—the age of its fleets, some of the issues we had with manpower—and then to try to make a great first step in getting a strategy right and bringing those factors into balance. What we'll probably get from this QDR, at least from this first phase, will be a solid recognition of that imbalance, and procedures will be put into place to get the strategy right and then an effort to continue QDR to get the structure and the resources into check. The balance is key to us.

"The second thing is kind of a subset of the first," he said. "Since Desert Storm, some would say, our missions have gone up 200 to 300 percent. The force is overextended. We're into enduring commitments. With the Sinai, it's now almost 20 years. We've been in Kuwait since '91. We've been in Bosnia almost six years. We go into places; we don't get out. We're committed around the world in small numbers, but this has compounding effects on the tempo of the force and the ability to retain and attract replacement personnel. As we work through that strategy/structure mismatch, the day-to-day obligation of forces has received an awful lot of attention from the team that's working this QDR. Part of the outcome will be to resolve some of the strains and stresses we've put on the force.

"We've probed questions that haven't been probed in quite

some time," Byrnes added. "One of the true strengths will be a real look at why we have forces where we have them. What are our commitments to smaller-scale contingencies? Why, and in what numbers? We're probing all the organizational constructs and platform programs that have been taken for granted.

"There is also a recognition that QDR is not an every-four-year event," he said. "Under the current administration we're going to see this as a continuous event. If we are truly going to transform, it's not a spot decision that we make in '01, and then move on. You're going to see a continuous effort to study and advance the ball in terms of transforming the force."

Byrnes concluded, "One of the things I do think we have to work on is the issue of trust—trust between the military and some of the civilian leadership. I'm not talking about the Secretary; I'm talking about the teams he had in place running this who spoke for him on a daily basis. We've got to restore that trust. If we split the services and their components apart the last time, this time we have more of an issue between the military and civilians. We've got to take action now to bring that back together."

He continued, "The story of the QDR will be that if we are going to transform the military, we're going to do it deliberately, over an extended period of time. It's not going to be a knee-jerk reaction to some of the expectations that might have been built up."

Q & A: How Does America Want to Use Its Unrivaled Power?

A print journalist offered a different assessment of Clinton and Bush.

"Clearly, what happened during the Clinton administration

was that budgets were cut by hundreds of millions of dollars at the same time missions were expanded; that was really the problem. Then, money was spent on things like environmental security so that while new ships were being cut up, the Pentagon was busy making the grass grow on military bases," he said.

"The problem is that the administration is coming in now to fix it," he said. "The way it was explained to me, from some pretty good sources, is that Rumsfeld went to the White House and ended up getting in a clash between politics and government. Apparently, he wanted to make these big increases and changes and was told basically, 'No, we need to get some points on the board with the American people,' and that the driving factor in the current administration now is to get re-elected. That may sound unusual, but I don't think it's unprecedented. And so the $40 billion in [defense budget] increases was reduced to $18 billion or so.

> **"The [Bush] administration's approach to the news media is fundamentally different from the Clinton administration's approach. I would characterize it as 'no news is good news.'"**

"The [Bush] administration's approach to the news media is fundamentally different from the Clinton administration's approach, which was spin-oriented," the reporter said. "They could make a jackass look like a racehorse, or a glass that was half-empty look half-full. The new administration's approach really comes from Cheney. I would characterize it as 'no news is good news.' They do not want to deal with news stories," he said.

"That's going to be a big problem for them, especially communicating on the big issues, especially missile defense. I don't see any kind of even modest public diplomacy effort for missile defense. And when they actually let the contract for the very first test facility in Alaska, they did it with an announcement in the *Federal Register.*

That's not exactly a major roll-out. So clearly they're going to have an uphill fight," he said.

McIntyre responded, "I don't think there's any debate that the cuts that took place around 1998 resulted in a real readiness problem. That was obvious when the chiefs all went up and testified and were allowed to tell the truth about how bad things were getting. My only point was that going into the campaign there was a realization that there was a problem in the military. Both candidates were operating under the realization there were some bills that were going to have to be paid by the new administration, whichever administration that was."

Crowley added, "The challenge for the news media is to get past the bumper stickers of political campaigns and get to the fact that there *are* real differences between what the Democrats proposed last year in the campaign and what President Bush is now committed to pursue. Bush did get a free ride during the campaign on many areas, in particular, in his National Press Club speech where he talked about strategic cuts. He was basically outlining the plan that existed with START III, down to 2,000 to 2,500 missiles. And yet it was portrayed as something different and more significant than had already been in existence. So it is important for you all to look past the campaign slogans.

"For example, the terminology 'pro-military' is bogus," he said. "I can't think of a president of the United States ever who wasn't pro-military and in one fashion or another didn't take care of the troops. If that feeds the perception that somehow Republicans can do defense, but Democrats can't do defense, that is not good for our country.

"Budget numbers are important, but sometimes in Washington we get so wrapped up in the numbers that we lose sight of what they mean," Crowley said. "There is a real difference between pursuing missile defense within a context of the ABM treaty and pursuing it while letting the ABM treaty lapse. There is a Republican theology on missile defense that is different from the Democratic approach to missile defense. That needs to be probed and understood. I'm not saying one side is right or wrong, but there is a clear difference.

"The issue on North Korea is very important," he said. "President Clinton ran out of time in trying to pursue an interim agreement that would freeze the North Korean missile program. The Bush administration did review the issue and has put some new conditions on the approach to negotiations with North Korea. That is a *big* deal. And how North Korea responds to that and how the Bush administration handles that issue has great implications, for example, in terms of the politics of missile defense," he said.

"These are the real issues," Crowley reiterated. "It is important for presidents who campaign to have to either adapt or support the positions they took during that campaign. But right now what is important is to get past who had what number and really study the strategic review, and then help the American people understand the implications for the future."

A radio journalist returned to the internal workings of the Defense Department: "Some very senior people in this administration, people I trust, tell me that Rumsfeld is really out of the loop, that the decisions on national defense are being made by two people at the White House—[National Security Adviser] Condoleezza Rice and [Vice President] Dick Cheney—and that Dick Cheney is the de facto Secretary of Defense."

Addressing himself to Quigley, he said, "At the same news conference where the Secretary talked about the lack of public awareness and/or support of the military, he did say something that I refer to as the Pontius Pilate approach, the washing of the hands. He said, 'Well, what we're going to do is give each of the services a certain amount of money and let each service decide what it plans to do with the money.' That sounds like a classic cop-out."

Quigley responded, "That's overly simplistic. If you're talking about defense planning guidance, and fiscal guidance, and stuff like that, they are much more specific about the sorts of capabilities and missions the services are expected to take on, although they do give considerable latitude as to how the services will then accomplish that capability, and they give them a budget top line.

"There will be plenty of time for debate as to specifically what systems and structures are the appropriate ones to put in place before the President's budget goes to the Congress. The defense planning guidance is not an end, it is a beginning," he said.

A senior Marine officer asked what will happen if the review shows that the new strategy will take a larger force structure than produced by the current policy, and "we still don't have any more money. Intuitively, I would expect it's going to take a larger force."

Quigley responded, "I don't know that there is an answer yet. The current thinking is that the force structure in the aggregate will be very comparable to what you see today. How it's equipped and how it is structured might be quite different, but I don't think it will end up being dramatically larger or smaller. If it is dramatically larger, then we're going to have to think about that again. I just don't think that's the expectation."

The Marine said the reason for all the talk about expectations for sweeping change is that "there's only so much money. So no matter how much Secretary Rumsfeld tried to depress expectations of radical change, elsewhere in the administration people had already decided you weren't going to get any more money. If they were going to stick to that, you needed the cuts. That's why the rhetoric about radical change kept popping up. You can't cut modernization. You can't cut readiness. The only place left to cut is force structure."

A print journalist said, "I'll admit to being as confused as everyone else about what sort of theoretical construct's going to come out of this. I have to laugh when someone complains and criticizes that the Clinton administration did these budget exercises, and made the strategy and the force fit the budget, and how terrible that was. Now we're going to change the strategy, but the force we're going to get out of that is going to be about the same force we have now, at about the same budget. We're doing the exact same thing we always do.

"What I have found useful is to say, 'Show me the money. Where is the money going to be?'" he said. "This is why these guys have gotten a pretty free ride. They campaigned on saving the military, but on a five-year budget plan that was less than Gore's. We know what it takes to save the military. We know that if the CBO [Congressional Budget Office] says it's $50 billion a year and Center for Strategic and International Studies says $100 billion a year, it's somewhere in between to fund and modernize this size force. Given that, it was a deathblow to their saving the military when they pushed the review off while they passed their tax cut, because that told you that defense was not a high priority with these guys. And once that tax cut was passed, the money's not going to be there to add to the top line to save the military. So you've got a $50-billion short-fall. They filled $18 billion of it, but the out years look very problematic.

"So how do you save the military?" he asked. "That's why it better be a radical, dramatic restructuring, because they can't fund this force at this level of money. Transformation really becomes a money-saving exercise. You'd better transform in a way that lets you either cut force structure, cut a number of major weapon systems, or cut what the military is being asked to do. They started out with 'OK, we're going to cut what the military is asked to do.' That's been a nonstarter. They haven't found any place that I've seen to really pull back from what the military's being asked to do."

The result, he pointed out, is that "we're getting down to the last two things, which are force structure and major weapons program. And if this QDR and this new strategy doesn't come up with those, then we're going to see the same thing we saw with the Clinton administration, which was, basically, watch the military continue to deteriorate slowly and try to fix it with rhetoric.

"The wild card is missile defense and what it will eventually cost," he said. "With the Clinton administration's very, very limited missile defense, we were talking $60 billion over the next 10 years— probably to rise to $100 billion if anything like traditional cost growth in these high-tech weapons programs comes to bear. These guys are talking about something much, much, much more elaborate. It's going to probably at least double the cost. That's $200 billion over the next 10 years. Bush has not explained at all where that money is coming from. I just look at the money, and I don't see a very rosy picture for the military."

The most fundamental question that hasn't been communicated and hasn't been answered is, what do we want to use America's unprecedented, unrivaled power for, now and in future years?

Another print reporter said communicating exactly what the administration would like to do is the Bush administration's biggest challenge.

"They want to find this extra money by reducing the growth in non-military programs, except for education. If so, they're going to have to do a hell of a lot better job communicating to the American people why they're going to take money out of energy, transportation, all these other areas they're going to need to raid in order to fund not just the $18 billion, but just to hold where we are. They're going to have to go up to something like $347, $348 billion next year," he said. "And that's without even counting missile defense. Where is that money going to come from?

"All of the leaks, the briefings, the backgrounders of any significance that are being done by the small, intimate groups that the

Secretary meets with are being done for media that is read inside the Beltway—*The Washington Post* and the *New York Times*. They're not read by the people who are going to put pressure on their congressmen to make the kind of changes this administration is going to press Congress to make.

"So it comes down to a very serious problem with communicating why they want these increases in defense, what they want these increases to fund, why we need transformation." He concluded, "more specifically, the most fundamental question that hasn't been communicated and hasn't been answered is, what do we want to use America's unprecedented, unrivaled power for, now and in future years? What is it that we want to achieve? What is our ultimate goal in international affairs, in using American power? And they haven't done that."

A television journalist added her opinion: "We failed to address the real, fundamental issue here, which is, what happens when there is a crisis? Because what is really going to grab the American people's attention and is going to make it matter to the U.S. military, to the administration, and to the media is when bullets start flying somewhere every six, eight, or 10 months, whether you need it or not. The American people expect that the U.S. military shoots back, and it's the U.S. military that wins. A lot of this is just, with all due respect, a lot of theoretical mumbo-jumbo, which goes out the door the second, God forbid, a U.S. pilot goes down in Iraq. Then we're all on our way to the airport, our lives all change, and the American people begin to look at the Bush administration with laser focus and look at the U.S. military with laser focus.

"What this whole first seven months of the Bush administration is about is a demonstration of their leadership and decision-making capability in a non-crisis atmosphere and how they might use it in a crisis atmosphere," she said. "The Chinese did Bush a big favor by letting the crew go. If that had gone on much longer, there would have been that type of laser focus. The Defense Secretary got lucky the first time in keeping his face away from the American public. In the next crisis, he won't get to do that. People are going to want to see him. They're going to want to see the joint chiefs. They're going to want to see the senior military leadership, and they're going to want to see decision-making capability that so far, in seven months, has failed to occur.

"Don Rumsfeld clearly is a cautious person who takes a lot of time to make a decision about anything and relies on a small group of people," she noted. "What we're going to be looking at in the media is how that decision-making process happens, because it's a proven fact, that when bullets are flying somewhere and the leadership relies on a very, very small group of people that is usually when they get into trouble. We're just in a waiting pattern until the next crisis occurs, and then we'll see what this all really means. At the moment, it's just a lot of words on paper."

A senior military officer summed up the dilemma: "It comes down to the allocation of resources and the competition for those resources. What helps you apportion resources wisely is a strategy. Not since the Roman Empire has a country so dominated the world politically, culturally, militarily, and economically as does America. The question is, where are we going? What is our national security strategy?"

Chapter 4
Military Investigations: Major Flashpoints

Many of the major recent flashpoints in the military-media relationship have involved a military investigation of some sort. Frustrations have plagued both sides.

For journalists, these investigations are major news. They need information immediately and do not want to (or cannot) wait for a slow, careful process to unfold. And they often may not understand the special rules and restrictions the military faces.

The military is bound by rules of law, ethics, and morality concerning the release of information during an investigation. During the investigation, the military gathers and analyzes evidence and information. While military people may want to release some information, their main concern is to avoid jeopardizing the investigation or those involved. In addition, all four services have different rules on the release of information about investigations; often, even military people do not understand their own rules.

Predictably, problems arise. If journalists do not have ready access to specific information, they may make mistakes by relying on those who can speak and speculate—retired officers, for example. Members of the active military, bound by rules that prevent them from releasing information, can all too easily look as if they are stonewalling or unwilling to provide information. In the tussle, the public, and the truth, can be the losers. Stories can go out that are unverified and may well prove to be wrong. Other important stories remain untold.

Many of the issues that play out during military investigations mirror the bigger-picture pattern that crops up again and again in the military-media relationship: each side accuses the other of not understanding its needs and constraints.

To provide a background for mutual understanding of the problems involved in coverage of investigations, a panel presented its views about military investigations:

• Michael Suessmann, retired Department of Defense (DOD) Assistant Inspector General (IG) for Departmental Inquiries, described what happens in cases involving senior military officials.

• Adm. Thomas Fargo, Commander of the U.S. Pacific Fleet, discussed the furor that resulted after the sinking of a Japanese fishing boat by the USS Greeneville.

• Attorney Charles Gittins drew from his extensive experience representing military personnel in courts martial to critique the military justice system and press coverage of it.

• Jim Schwenk, DOD's Associate Deputy Counsel, gave an overview of how the military justice system works.

• The Baltimore Sun's Tom Bowman *assessed the issues raised during press coverage of military investigations.*

Michael Suessmann, longtime Defense Department investigator, recalled a comment made at an earlier Cantigny Conference by Gen. Ronald Fogleman: "You lose the moral imperative to lead if you lose people's confidence that you are telling the truth."

This statement "serves to define the importance of all investigations conducted by the Department of Defense: get the facts so that the truth about the matter will be known," Suessmann said.

Suessmann focused on senior official cases, where the actions or decisions of general or flag officers, senior executive service officials, and senior presidential appointees are at issue. Such cases are challenging for both the Defense Department and the media, yet they are very important, because the outcome is viewed, both inside and outside, as affecting the credibility and reputation of the organization, he said.

"We all know it is difficult for any organization to critically examine the actions of its leaders or to objectively look at issues that go to its core values," Suessmann said. "We've seen this recently with the FBI [Federal Bureau of Investigation], as well as with Bridgestone-Firestone, and the tobacco companies. In DOD, it's even more complex because of additional pressures to make senior official cases go away as quickly and quietly as possible. [There are] the pressures of friendship, cases in which the people having to decide how to resolve a particular matter have a history with the official whose actions are under scrutiny. Pressures from the Hill, especially where the official has formed relationships with members of Congress or their staffs. The general politicizing of matters, such as the sexual harassment cases. And, not least, the unique and hierarchical nature of the military culture, including, ironically, the need for subordinates to have confidence in their leaders."

Because these cases are resolved administratively at the top level of the department or military service, there generally is no appeal process. He said, "That fact, coupled with all the environmental pressures, should cause you to suspect, correctly, that the disposition of these cases is more open to potential whitewashing or, rarely, anointing of a sacrificial lamb, than cases involving only lower-ranking personnel."

Suessmann criticized the media for "all too often merely summarizing the investigative reports and describing the actions taken." in the cases he handled. "Almost never would the media seek to identify the internal politics and atmospherics that led to the final result. The media did not question cases of obvious over-punishment or those that might reasonably be seen as under-punishment. Simply put, the media did not provide the sunshine necessary to keep the system honest in all cases."

Nevertheless, he asserted, "For the past 10 years, DOD, to its credit, has had in place probably the best structure in the federal government for conducting inquiries into allegations involving its senior officials. In 1991, then-Secretary [of Defense] Dick Cheney acted to change existing practices that had kept the whole story from being known. DOD started to require that each service ensure that all allegations received against a senior official were promptly reported to that service's Inspector General [IG], and, in turn, to the DOD IG. DOD IG exercised a right of first refusal to investigate any case or to defer to the service IG, subject to DOD's review of the final report.

"In practice," Suessmann said, "we told the military IGs that in order to conduct senior official investigations in *their* services, the work must be done by members of the service IG's own staff and that the office had to do credible work. This ended the practice of having matters locally investigated, often poorly, and locally resolved, often inappropriately."

This approach had two beneficial byproducts, he said: "First, the service chiefs or their vice chiefs became the decision-makers regarding administrative discipline of their generals or admirals. Second, all pending and completed inquiries would thereafter be known to the headquarters and the Hill for due consideration when an officer was up for another star."

Another goal of the program was to ensure transparency in investigations. "Before 1990, too often senior officials had defended themselves before all-too-receptive immediate commanders on the basis that the investigator's notes were wrong, that the investigator took a statement out of context, or that the guy doing the investigation just didn't understand what the senior official was talking about," Suessmann recalled. "To counter this, we required that all interviews be taped and transcribed. Since we started this practice, the 'they misquoted me' defense has disappeared."

Acknowledging that DOD's process, like anything else involving people, is subject to all the normal human foibles, he said that "nowhere is this more clear than in our examination into the Navy's mishandling of its own investigations in Tailhook. We found that the head of naval aviation was trying to protect his boys; the head of the naval investigative service didn't want to harm an operational relation between this and the aviators; the Navy IG didn't speak up to correct a dysfunctional relation that the IG had; and the undersecretary didn't challenge the actions of his professionals. And the whole investigative process was overlaid with a desire to do damage control to protect the Navy's reputation. In so doing, these senior officials confused what was good for them personally with what was good for the Navy. Just as at sea or in the air, sunshine is mostly good; fog is mostly bad."

Suessmann said another case merits mention "because it shows how a minor issue became a major flap due to poor work by public affairs offices. A *Newsweek* reporter received complaints that space-available travelers were denied seats on an Air Mobility Command C141-B aircraft flight from Naples, Italy to Colorado Springs, even though the plane was not full. Air Force Gen. Joseph W. Ashy and an aide were the only passengers on board. Following up, the reporter, joined by an ABC producer, got the runaround from Air Force public affairs offices at Space Command and Air Mobility Command as well as from the head office in the Pentagon. Colorado tried to foist the matter onto Scott Air Force Base, and vice versa, neither recognizing that there were larger Air Force interests to be considered. Equally important, neither provided timely corrections when it became known to them that they had given out incorrect information. The teaching point is that had the public affairs folks done a better job, the story would have been relatively mundane."

Summing up, Suessmann said, "Our workload was about 300 cases a year, between cases done by my office and those done by service IGs with our review of the final product. On average, in about 80 percent of those cases, we found no misconduct or impropriety. The media were unaware of the vast majority of our cases that cleared an official of the allegations made against him. I felt very strongly that an officer could expect some privacy in that regard and that the privacy interests of an official who had been *cleared* of the charges against him outweighed the man-bites-dog nature of such a story."

Military Responsibilities and Media Demands In Investigations

Adm. Thomas Fargo, commander of the Pacific Fleet, provided the commander's perspective in military investigations, using the *USS Greeneville* case as an example. "Certainly, the military, like any public entity, has an inherent obligation to keep the public informed," he began. "When we look at the *Greeneville* investigation, the end state had to be that the Japanese and the American public had a full accounting of the entire accident. But how you get there is really important, and there are a number of factors you have to keep in mind."

Some of those factors, Fargo noted, are the fleet commander's perspective, his responsibilities as the convening authority, the responsibilities of the investigating officers and the president of the court of inquiry, and the rights of the named parties who are subject to the investigation. "But ultimately what I've got to do is get to the facts and apply some corrective action to the situation to ensure that we have taken care of our primary responsibilities of good order and discipline and that we've improved the force," he said.

Noting that the first objective is to get the facts, Fargo said, "We'd like to do that as quickly as possible, but remember that the first reports are generally going to be poor. We learn this lesson day in and day out. They'll certainly be incomplete, but speed is important because we want to make sure we've taken action to ensure we don't have another incident of a similar nature."

The end state has to be...a full accounting of the entire accident. But how you get there is really important.

He said this drives the move toward a preliminary investigation (PI), which, he noted, "is a somewhat closed event. By *somewhat* I mean press information can be provided along the way, but the bulk of the investigation is going to be kept in a closed forum. The PI has a number of parts to it, but what I'm really looking for at this point is what we have here. I need this thing scoped to some degree. This will also set up the follow-on steps that could allow us to wrap up the investigation in total, or it could lead to a formal command investigation, or, as in the case of the *Greeneville*, actually lead to a court of inquiry.

"It's important to understand what we're telling our people in the wake of any accident," Fargo said. "From day one, when you walk on your first ship, we've told each sailor that if we have a problem, if there *is* an accident, you need to step forward with the facts for the sake of your shipmates and for the safety of your ship. It's part of our core values; we can't operate our ships or aircraft without the whole story. So admitting mistakes up front is a key part of our ethic."

He continued, "I said *somewhat* closed because we do want to provide facts along the way to the American public and keep them informed. That was the reason we conducted a press conference within 24 hours of the *Greeneville* incident, actually before she returned to port that next morning.

"What we didn't know that Saturday morning was that civilians had actually been at the controls," Fargo said. "We had provided during the press conference the fact that an emergency blow had taken place, that there were 16 civilians on board, but we didn't know at that point that they had participated in these procedures. When we did learn that, we didn't move quickly enough to get the information out. I think Jamie McIntyre and CNN broke that story before the Navy got to the chalkboard. In retrospect, that was clearly a mistake.

"If getting to the facts is the first step, preserving our ability to fix accountability is clearly the second and most important."

"I've become a believer in the press statement," he said. "Background has a place, response to query has a place, but the press statement becomes more and more valuable, especially when you're dealing with large media-interest items. That's why you saw a press statement on *Greeneville* on a relatively minor incident yesterday, because it provides clarity and allows the Navy to get on record at an early point.

"If getting to the facts is the first step," he said, "preserving our ability to fix accountability is clearly the second and most important. This is a fundamental purpose of the military justice system. At the end of the day, if the judgment can't be concluded properly or punishment can't be assigned if appropriate because we've mishandled the legal rights of the parties, then I'm going to create a larger long-term problem for my organization. So you've got to deal with the issues of personal accountability in a particularly sensitive manner. We all know what command influence is. Savvy lawyers use it, and rightfully so. Cases are thrown out for reasons of command influence, and that's bad for the fleet. It's no way to maintain account-ability, and it erodes public confidence in our institution.

"Because of this, investigation becomes a little more deliber-ate," Fargo said. "This is different from a safety or mishap review like the NTSB [National Transportation Safety Board] does. Of course, in the *Greeneville* case, the NTSB was up every night talking about what they had learned or what they surmised. But the NTSB is charged with finding out the safety implications of the accident; they have no responsibilities whatsoever in determining accountability."

The final responsibility of the commander is the integrity of the investigation, he said. "It was important to me that this investigation be correct and proper. That's the fundamental reason that I elected to go to a court of inquiry, which was a totally open process."

Fargo explained, "There were lots of different pieces to this: the conduct of the captain, the crew, the operating area, the distin-guished visitors, the embarked senior officers. My concern was that if we went to a standard command investigation and the public had no insight into the investigation, given the level of interest and the complexity of the incident, it would naturally be met with suspicion. They would challenge the integrity of the investigation; there would be a perception that there was more to the story, no matter what the conclusion of a closed investigation might be.

"So, very frankly, that's the reason we elected that particular path," he said. "I had no idea how the court of inquiry would come out. We hadn't done one in 12 years in the Navy, but I felt that the visibility and the transparency would provide public confidence, and it would provide confidence in the fleet also in terms of the determinations we made—that we had gotten to the bottom of this.

"You can't do a court of inquiry often," Fargo said. "It took a huge amount of resources. Just dealing with the 450 credentialed press we had in Hawaii was a huge effort. It takes a great deal of time to bring this all together. If we went that route in every investigation, it would bring the Navy to all-stop."

Regarding the media and the public, he said, "There's no doubt we learned a lot along the way. Six months later, looking back at *Greeneville*, I feel pretty good about where we ended up. We did get the entire story out. It was an open process. I felt pretty good essentially after the first week, when we had made the decision to go that particular route.

"There was a great deal of hullabaloo the first week that, in retrospect, I think was driven largely by the press' desire for the names of the 16 civilians on board," he recalled. "You all felt there was a large story there, maybe a Lincoln bedroom-like story. As it turned out, there wasn't. I wouldn't release the names at that point because the preliminary investigation was still in progress. I didn't yet know the civilians' relationship to the accident; I needed to get to the facts. I thought releasing the names would make that more difficult, and certainly there were privacy issues involved. Once the preliminary investigation was completed and we were moving to an open process, I didn't have any problems releasing those names. I think in the aftermath, we got that one right, but I'd have to tell you it was an awfully painful week."

Fargo made four points.

"The first is maximum disclosure and minimum delay, getting the word out early," Fargo said. "I've mentioned the press conference we conducted that first Saturday, the day after the accident. You have to expect that you're going to get some bum dope in those first days, because the information comes from initial reports.

"I'm reminded of when Adm. Crowe [William J. Crowe Jr., former Chairman of the Joint Chiefs of Staff] stepped forward the first day after the Vincennes and Iranian airbus incident and told people essentially all that he knew," Fargo said. "As we know now, most of what he provided turned out not to be accurate. But he got high marks for telling what he knew to be the situation as reported at that particular time. It's also essential, of course, that the commander not be speculative or provide opinion because it does affect the integrity of the investigation. Subjective or speculative analysis by a uniformed officer is a danger to our ability to affix accountability in the end."

The second lesson he learned from the *Greeneville* incident concerned what he called the "center of gravity" of the media.

"When I stepped out that first Saturday, I thought the center of gravity was in Hawaii; I thought I was speaking to the entire world. In retrospect, though the story broke on Friday, by Saturday, a lot of you had left for the weekend, our Chief of Information staff was back in their office trying to work out where they were going to go on this, and much of what I said wasn't covered. On Monday morning, the center of gravity certainly wasn't in Hawaii. It was where you folks were, where the concentration of media, of people with a solid knowledge of military proceedings, and the analysts were. Eventually, it became very clear that with two separate points on the globe in parallel we wouldn't get the story out properly.

"The third point we learn day in and day out is that the Navy has to have experts who can and will talk," he said. "The media, both in Hawaii and certainly back east, had to produce a story whether we were there to help them or not. There was a large degree of interest, and the civilian audience doesn't readily understand all that we do, especially when it has to do with the submarine force. So you've got to place people, uniformed where possible, but retired where necessary, who can provide expert opinion. If you don't, the media will go to folks who are either less knowledgeable or who have a different agenda. I saw that on any number of occasions—people who stepped forward who were so far detached or dated from the situation that they really couldn't provide useful information. In some cases it was actually embarrassing. We found a team of experts was necessary, and that's what we provided to the media center.

"The last piece is dealing with large media interest," he said. "This requires a tremendous commitment of personnel and resources. You can't do it all on background by any stretch of the imagination. Things like Web pages where you can post information on a regular basis are hugely important. I found the Japanese press, given an opportunity to get it wrong, would. In one case, we stepped forward and said, 'We will conduct a search until we've exhausted all possibilities.' It was translated to, 'We'll search until we get tired.' Press releases that are formal in nature, formal press conferences, and briefings were key to dealing with the sheer magnitude of the press and getting the word out."

Defender of the People

Charles Gittins, a veteran defense attorney in military cases, made his perspective clear: "I defend the *people*. I'm not really concerned with the organization as much as Adm. Fargo and others are. My job is to represent my client, get him through the military investigative process, and, hopefully, show him that there's light at the other end of the tunnel, that he's going to have a life after the proceedings are over.

"When I was still on active duty, I was the investigating officer on a friendly-fire incident that happened in Desert Storm, where a Marine A-6 bombed an artillery column," he recalled. "I was assigned to it because I was a judge advocate and a former aviator. Although I didn't talk to Gen. [Walter] Boomer [former Assistant Commandant of the Marine Corps] personally, the importance was impressed upon me by his Chief of Staff and my boss that the investigation be entirely accurate and that we get to the bottom of things. It turned out that a bombardier navigator and a pilot weren't paying attention to what they were doing, and they injured some fellow Marines. That was a bad thing, but the investigation was complete; we got to the bottom of it, and it was a very full report.

"When I left active duty, I went to Williams & Connolly in Washington, D.C.," Gittins said. "Virtually the first thing I did was represent Bob Stumpf in the Tailhook investigation. That was my first experience with the press. Bob Stumpf became the poster boy for Tailhook. There was a great deal of press interest in his case because he was legally and factually innocent, but, nonetheless, the Secretary of the Navy wouldn't promote him to captain."

"The last thing I want in a case is press attention. It tends to drive the direction of the case to a degree that is not good for the client."

Gittins had experience with a number of military investigations: in the cable car incident in Cavalese, Italy, he represented one of the passengers on the EA-6B Prowler jet who ultimately did not go to trial because he had nothing to do with flying the airplane. Gittins also represented Army Sgt. Maj. Gene McKinney in his court martial. And he represented 42 midshipmen in the Naval Academy's cheating scandal.

"So I come to the table with some experience in high-visibility investigations, and I will tell you, *I do not like the press*," he said. "The last thing I want in a case is press attention. It tends to drive the direction of the case to a degree that is not good for the client and not good for the institution. However, I recognize that that's the way it is in the United States. The press has an interest in covering events of national importance, and you have to deal with them.

"My concern from the point of view of representing people is that the investigation be competent and that it be done in a timely but correct manner," Gittins said. "'If you want it bad, you get it bad' is an old adage. Speed is not the most important thing. Accuracy is the most important thing, particularly when the individual at the other end of the disciplinary process is a long-term military member who has given great service to his country.

"That said, my experience has been that the legal process and the investigative process that have been set up by the military services are good processes," he remarked. "When they get changed for a particular case, that should be of concern to everyone. And I don't think the press picks up on that.

"For example, in the Naval Academy case, a well-organized honor process was essentially thrown out the window and a process that was created ad hoc was substituted for it," Gittins said. "As a matter of policy, the investigators decided they would not read military members their Article 31 rights: the right to remain silent and to have a lawyer there. They demanded that those midshipmen— young, 22-, 21-year-olds—basically incriminate themselves. The policy decision was, 'Well, we're not going to use the information at courts martial.' Article 31 doesn't say you've got to give a military member their rights for purposes of court martial. It says if you suspect them of an offense, you have to read them their rights. So, as a matter of policy, Navy officials decided they were going to violate the rights of more than 100 midshipmen. That is of concern to a lawyer who represents people."

Using the McKinney court martial as an example, Gittins said, "I'm a firm believer that the criminal investigation should be private, should be conducted by professional investigators, and then should be given to the commander and he should make his decision. It should not be bandied about in the press: the witnesses shouldn't be talking to the press, and we shouldn't see witnesses on TV talking about the issues in a criminal case. Criminal investigation needs to be conducted confidentially, and the results need to be competent and provided to the commander."

However, he continued, "once you get to the formal fact-finding process, court martial, or whatever, *that* process needs to be entirely transparent to the public, for constitutional reasons, for one—the right to a public trial. Once again, in the McKinney case, as his civilian lawyer and lead counsel, we became concerned when the Article 32 investigation was closed.

"Now, there was some case law that Article 32 could be closed for child witnesses—children who are talking about abuse—but the McKinney case involved adults who were claiming sexual misconduct by the Sergeant Major of the Army," Gittins said. "That needed to be public. They needed to be able to make those allegations in public.

"When the command decided to close the Article 32 investigation in its entirety, that was of grave concern to me," he said. "I suspected that due process would have gone out the window. So we went to the court of appeals for the armed forces, along with ABC News, and now we have a law that basically says that Article 32 investigations are open and if you're going to close them, you'd better have a good reason.

"It turned out for Gene McKinney that the Article 32 investigation was the reason he was acquitted of 18 of 19 counts of sexual misconduct at his trial, because that investigation, once the court weighed in, became a true fact-finding hearing," Gittins said. "It was used as discovery by me and his other lawyers to learn everything we could about those allegations. And we were able to provide substantial evidence at trial that showed some of them couldn't even have happened when they said they did or in the way they said they did.

"I'm convinced if that had been a closed hearing, it would have been about a three- or four-day ordeal," he said. "We would have learned virtually nothing. We probably wouldn't have had much in the way of witnesses. They would have called witness-availability issues and done it on paper. As it turned out, we ended up with witnesses who sat in the chair and were cross-examined, some for multiple days. But it was a transparent process to the public, it was fair to Gene McKinney, it was fair to the Army, and we got to the right result ultimately in the court martial."

Turning to his defense of Scott Waddle in the *Greeneville* case, Gittins said, "The reason I get called, I believe, is because, since 1987, I've done nothing but military justice, representing military people in courts martial and administrative matters. Unfortunately, the experience level for Navy lawyers, Marine lawyers, is low. They don't have the caseload that supports a lot of experience. So, a couple weeks into the event, I got called by Scott Waddle. I said, 'The court of inquiry is scheduled for a week from now. I can't be there; I've got another trial. Let's put in a request for continuance. But in the meantime, I would suggest you be thinking about who you want to represent you.'

"It was a transparent process to the public, it was fair to Gene McKinney, it was fair to the Army, and we got to the right result ultimately in the court martial."

"He indicated who his Navy lawyers were," Gittins said. "One of his lawyers had not tried a case in a number of years, and the lawyer was a claims officer who adjudicated claims. That gave him some concern; he wanted a *trial* lawyer. So I gave him the names of a couple of lawyers I thought were pretty good Navy lawyers, who had a lot of experience. He made a request, which was his right under those procedures, for a very experienced lawyer who *was* available, and who was actually serving as a defense counsel. It was denied.

"When we ultimately got the denial, there was some concern on our part because Scott's request for an individual military counsel who happened to be assigned to Norfolk was denied, but another officer's request for an individual military counsel who was located in Mayport was approved," he recalled. "The rules permitted a denial for reasons of non-availability, meaning, the lawyer's not located in the same judicial circuit. But if the lawyer in Norfolk wasn't available for Scott Waddle, how could another lawyer also out of the judicial circuit be available for another officer?

"So now we have what looks to be an arbitrary decision," Gittins said. "Then we learned that the procedures were going to change for the court of inquiry. There's a regulation for courts of inquiry. You pull the regulation out; it tells you exactly how it's done. The members of the court of inquiry have to be federal employees or active-duty officers, and there's also a provision that allows for expert advisers to the court of inquiry with no similar limitation on their qualifications. We were told we were going to have a Japanese rear admiral as a member of the panel. 'He's not going to vote,' they said, 'but he will deliberate, and you can't challenge him for cause.'

"Once again, they're changing the rules, because the rules are that you can challenge the members for cause, you can challenge any adviser to the board for cause," he said.

"At any rate, procedures were changed," Gittins said. "Did it come out right? Yes. The court of inquiry, I believe, was a fair proceeding, ultimately, and it was transparent to the public, which was good, transparent to the Japanese."

In conclusion, referring to Fargo's remarks, Gittins said after an accident or during an investigation, the Navy expects that people who are involved will make statements or talk about the issue, and the person may face prosecution later. In a normal aircraft crash, the pilot who makes a mistake is unlikely to be prosecuted. He may be sued civilly, but he's not going to be prosecuted. "Despite the fact that you want to get to the bottom of things, you still have to respect military members' rights. That's the bottom line. The fact that the press wants answers or the fact that the military needs answers should not justify overriding military members' rights," Gittins said.

What Are the Rules, and Why?

Jim Schwenk, DOD's associate deputy counsel, focused his remarks on the rules for military investigations, why they exist, and where they come from.

"The basic reason for the rules is to make sure that people get a fair trial," he said. "Any time you have an incident, immediately the thought is, is somebody accountable, and, if so, how are they going to be held accountable? And is a trial or any other kind of adverse proceeding a possibility? So we look carefully at how to ensure a fair trial. The American Bar Association does that; the Association of District Attorneys, the Justice Department, and U.S. attorneys throughout the country do that. They have rules that apply in these kinds of situations.

"We follow basically the civilian ethical rules that govern what you're supposed to say and not say. But there is a difference," Schwenk said. "As much as there is a parallel, there is a fundamental difference on the issue of fairness between your local DA [district attorney], the U.S. attorney, and the commander. The difference is unlawful command influence. Unlawful command influence is a unique aspect of military justice that is, according to the five civilians who sit on the Court of Appeals of the Armed Forces, our senior appellate court, the mortal enemy of military justice. And it is what every lawyer brings into every meeting.

"When that plane hit the gondola in Italy and 20 people died, the first thing I talked to my general about in Norfolk was unlawful command influence," he recalled. "At the same time, I talked to the CINC's [Commander-in-Chief] lawyer in Europe, and one of the first items on his agenda was unlawful command influence. And the commandant's lawyers were talking to the commandant about unlawful command influence. If you know Gen. Krulak [Gen.

Charles C. Krulak, Commandant of the Marine Corps], you know they had the most difficult job of all. We focused on that all along the chain of command because in a worst-case situation you end up at a court martial and the defense lawyer, Charlie Gittins, raises unlawful command influence.

"What is unlawful command influence?" he asked. "It occurs when a commander by what he says or does tends to indicate how he wants things to develop. For example, you might have a court martial involving drugs. Your service chief, the commandant of the Marine Corps, might come down on a visit to the command, where he has a get-together with all his officers. He talks about policies, about the drug policy, and says something like, 'Drugs are bad; we can't have drugs.' The members of the court martial are there because they're officers. They then go to sit on the court martial. That's a reported case. And the court had no trouble saying 'unlawful command influence.'"

Schwenk continued, "Did the commandant know those guys sitting on the court were in the audience? No. Was he perfectly within bounds talking about his policy and the Marine Corps' policy on drugs? Yes. Did it have an adverse effect on the military justice process? Yes. And so the court said, 'We can't let this court martial proceed. Go find some other members and start over again.'"

Noting that almost anything a commander says or does can create unlawful command influence, Schwenk pointed out that this "leads to a situation where there is a lack of candor on the part of the government. It is for what we think is a good reason. Charlie cannot commit unlawful command influence. If he thinks it's in the best interest of his client to get out there and talk to the media, he will. Any good defense counsel will go out there and do that, and there will be an imbalance. This causes a problem for the media, because you're getting one side of the story, and you're thinking, 'I wonder how up-front these guys really are. What else is out there?' So you go, as you always do, to the other side, and we tell you, 'Sorry, I can only go so far, and no farther.' How are you going to report that? What are you going to say? It causes a problem. But there's a good reason for the problem; it may well be one of the tensions in the system that's designed to be there.

"The other thing besides a fair trial that everybody worries about is this law that Congress, on behalf of the American people and the president, decided ought to be in effect for federal employees, the Privacy Act," he said. Military and civilian employees can be sued if they reveal adverse information about other government employees that is covered by the Privacy Act. "They knew full well when they passed this act that it was going to get in the way of candor to the American people about all sorts of things."

They knew full well when they passed this act that it was going to get in the way of candor to the American people about all sorts of things.

He listed some things DOD can talk about: "Obviously, we'll tell you the name, grade, age, unit, regular duty station, regular duties at the duty station, the general nature of the offenses, name of the victim if it's not a sex offense, name of the defense counsel, who's doing the investigation, when they were picked up, if they are in the brig or in confinement, where they are in confinement. That, for sure, will always go out, or should always go out. But that doesn't give you much.

"Now it's time to dig in and find out what all this really means," Schwenk said. "Who said what to whom? Why do we think this happened? What are the effects? That's where you run into worrying about a fair trial."

What *can't* DOD talk about? "We don't talk about the prior criminal record of the accused. Pretty obvious: 'If he did it before, he must have done it again.' Confessions, admissions, and alibis, or a refusal to talk when presented with the opportunity. 'We'd like to know what's going on too, but he won't talk to us. Gittins got to him first.' We don't say that. Scientific tests or refusal to take scientific tests, or the results of tests.

"We don't talk about witnesses, which goes back to Adm. Fargo's comments about the civilians on board the *Greeneville*," Schwenk pointed out. "We don't talk about their identity, testimony, or their credibility. The reason is, if people can talk to witnesses and then all of a sudden we have witness problems, the credibility of the investigation can be put at risk.

He added, "We don't talk about pretrial negotiations or what a person is going to plead until it actually gets into open court and goes out into the public. We don't talk about anything else that could adversely affect the integrity of the process for the good of the accused, or potential accused, and the good of the institution. That's the list.

"There can be exceptions," Schwenk said. "We do have rules that say we can talk about these kinds of things when there are exceptional circumstances, where the information is already out there, where there's some kind of reason. But it's got to be a pretty compelling reason before you do it. So sometimes we do release information, but the basic bias, for the reasons I expressed—fair trial, avoiding unlawful command influence and complying with the Privacy Act—is not to release that kind of information."

Finally, Schwenk pointed out, "the media are not alone in the limit on what they get access to. We have a very firm policy all the way through the attorney general and the president not to make people who do military justice decision-making available for questioning. That includes the GAO [General Accounting Office] and Congress. You can imagine how well it goes down when we don't make them available, but we don't. We're willing to assert executive privilege. The president will assert executive privilege to restrict these people from going over and answering questions about the deliberative process. They can talk about all sorts of other things, as Adm. Fargo did here today, but we think it is so important to keep the personal judgment of that individual untrammeled by unlawful command influence, whether from the executive branch or the legislative branch, which pass on their promotions, that we don't make them available to discuss their deliberative process—why they reached the decision they reached in a disposition of a case."

A Media Critique of Military Investigations

Tom Bowman, military affairs reporter for the *Baltimore Sun,* said the military-media relationship varies greatly with the circumstances.

"The press and the military can execute a beautiful tango together when it's in their interests. Or it can be like an Irish divorce: we're both in the same house, but we just don't talk to each other," he said.

"We've seen the beautiful tango recently with stories like 'Are they going to cut two Army divisions, and what effect will that have?' And, 'Are aircraft carriers vulnerable to missile attacks? Are they dinosaurs? Should we get rid of them?' At times like this you'll see the services more than willing to deal with the press to get the message out to try to maybe prevent others from doing some damage," he said.

"Outside of war or major conflict, it's probably during investigations where you see serious problems between military and the press," Bowman said. "And sometimes it's not even an Irish divorce. I would say it's an eye-gouging street fight to try to get information.

"In any investigations we've talked about, from the cheating scandal at the Naval Academy up to the *Greeneville*, what you hear a lot of times from military people is, 'You folks are just trying to sell newspapers. And who the hell appointed you as arbiters of what's right and what's wrong?' My response would be that we perform an important and vital role in this country. We don't always do it right. We screw up too much. But it's the founding fathers who enshrined us in the First Amendment, and they did that for a reason. They wanted the press to be a watchdog over government and what the government does with our money, and how government officials act, and what is done in our name.

We perform an important and vital role in this country. We don't always do it right. We screw up too much. But it's the founding fathers who enshrined us in the First Amendment, and they did that for a reason.

"We are a pain in the neck. Some have an even lower opinion of us," Bowman said. "It's the investigations that are really the hallmark of what we do when they're done right. If you look at the investigations over the years that have involved the military—the My Lai Massacre, Tailhook, Mark Thompson's great work on helicopter troubles, and Pat Sloyan, who told us more about the Gulf War after it was over than we learned during the war— these are really important investigations. They're painful at the time, and we get criticized a lot, but they tend to make the institutions stronger, when all is said and done.

"If I could send one message today it's that what we need from the military in these investigations is information as quickly as possible," he emphasized. "A lot of times we'll call the public affairs people and say we need the information yesterday. And with the frenzy of an investigation like the *Greeneville* and with the 24-hour news cycle these days, it's very difficult to get the information quickly. But certainly with the *Greeneville* incident, the information that civilians were at the controls should have been put out faster than it was."

Bowman added, "Another thing I would suggest is that the military try as much as possible to put forward experts when something *does* break, to explain what an emergency ballast blow is, and what the proper periscope search is, so we're not running off to folks who have been retired 20 or 30 years to try to get the answers. A lot of times we'll go to press conferences and the person doing the brief will just say, 'I really don't know.' If we need the information quickly, it would be in everyone's interest to have experts available, whether it's a historian talking about the Korean War and No Gun Ri, or someone who can say, 'I was a skipper of a sub, and this is the procedure.' You don't have to second guess what the skipper did or didn't do in the incident, but you can at least tell us, 'This is how it's supposed to work.'"

He also commented on how information is passed to the press: "Jamie McIntyre made a good point in a recent Freedom Forum piece about when the Apaches [helicopters] were downed in Albania and how the Army released the information. They slipped a note under his door at 9:30 at night. That's just unacceptable. That kind of thing really sows distrust between us and makes the Irish divorce even worse."

Reviewing some recent investigations, Bowman said, "In the Aberdeen scandal, the Army did a pretty good job getting information out, which is remarkable, because a lot of us usually have trouble trying to get information from the Army. But that time they really rose to the occasion and did a pretty good job. They got the information out and set in motion corrective actions about drill sergeants, and how they are trained and selected, and so forth.

"The key with any investigation is, get the information out, do a mea culpa if need be, come up with corrective action and move on," Bowman said. "That's the only way to do it. If you withhold information, and it trickles out, as did the information about the *Greeneville*, it's going to sow distrust between the press and the military. But even more, it's going to make the institution look bad. I had neighbors coming up to me saying, 'Why were civilians driving the submarine?' That was the perception—that they were actually driving the boat. Who does that hurt? It hurts the Navy; you look foolish."

He continued, "I don't think the Army did a very good job with No Gun Ri. The AP [Associated Press] did a wonderful job of looking into that, though it's still a bit murky. Certainly people died, but were orders given? The Army's response was to have the Center for Military History look into it. For some reason, the Center for Military History couldn't tell the press through the Army's spokesman whether these units were even at the bridge at that time, which I found unbelievable. And the Secretary of the Army, when this whole thing broke, greets the press by saying, 'I only have time for a few questions. I have an appointment.' I mean, give me a break. He took several questions and basically said, 'We don't know what's going on. We don't know where the units were at the time.' Then he marched out the door. The Army looked ridiculous.

"With the Navy, Adm. Fargo has already said there are things they could have done better, and I think on the Naval Academy cheating scandal, I would give the Navy mixed reviews," Bowman said. "They did a pretty good job getting information out, but a lot of the information we got came from the Hill, which was maybe more forthcoming and keeping an eye on what was going on. That was a long and painful process. There were allegations that the superintendent at that time was trying to protect football players, though I don't think the Navy was.

"Charlie Gittins raised a good point," he added. "We should have done a little more on Article 31 rights at that time. We did mention it in passing, but in hindsight, we should have done more about whether the midshipman's rights were protected. Did they follow procedures or not follow procedures? And what Mike Suessmann had to say about investigations and getting to the politics of what goes on behind the scenes is another good point.

"Overall we have to do a better job at what we do, not only in investigations, but in day-to-day stories as well, because not only is it the *right* thing to do, it also shows the military that you're fair and accurate and you're doing your job," Bowman said. "Some of the Vieques coverage could have been better. It's now turned into more of a David vs. Goliath story, more of a political story, and there's rarely any mention about what the military says is necessary—that the range is necessary, that combined live-fire training is necessary for readiness. That issue has been lost."

As an example, Bowman described a radio report he heard: "They let one of the activists down in Vieques ramble on about how the range and the bombing is causing cancer in our children, and heart trouble, and none of that has been proven. Johns Hopkins had done studies saying there's no evidence of this. But the reporter didn't even question this guy. It's a good story. It's the big bad government beating up on the Vieques residents. We've got to do a better job of questioning everybody, including the poor people of Vieques: 'Is this accurate? Where's your evidence?'

"On the other hand, the *Los Angeles Times* did a good story about Fort Sill in Oklahoma and how there have been more people killed there, certainly more than at Vieques, and how the bombing range is even closer to an inhabited area than the one in Vieques," Bowman said.

Bowman observed that in the *Greeneville* case, journalists were "tripping over each other" to get to Hawaii to cover it; some might have been education reporters or general assignment reporters "who don't know a submarine from an M-16. It's probably in the interests of military officers in the Pentagon to try—and this is self-serving, but I'm going to say it anyway—to deal with those who cover the military on a regular basis, the Pentagon press corps. It might have been better to drag us all into the room at the Pentagon and talk about the folks who were at the controls before you announced it to the 'Hawaiian press corps' or to the world."

Q & A: A Welter of Issues

A newspaperman raised the issue of the Osprey, noting that what led to disclosure of maintenance problems was the sending of a tape and letter by someone at New River to 60 *Minutes*.

"Does that indicate within the services a lack of confidence in the system itself and the people who are governed by that system?" he asked. "The way the Marines conducted the public relations aspect of that might even serve as a model of how to get information out quickly and accurately. But I wonder, if that tape and letter hadn't been sent, would that have happened? Would we have had the Marines conducting what I thought was an extremely responsible public relations operation connected to that investigation?"

Suessmann said, "There are regulations in the department to protect whistle-blowers. Based on the whistle-blower reprisal cases I and my folks investigated, yes, people become whistle-blowers when they don't trust their chain of command. And the government benefits from those whistle-blowers. It's unfortunate that people don't feel they can go forward in their chain of command, but there are cases when that just isn't doable, when the immediate chain of command, perhaps, is tainted by the matter at issue, as might be the case with the V-22."

Gittins said, "I don't know who leaked the tape, but that person may have been involved in criminal misconduct. If he was told that he had to falsify documents and did it knowing it was wrong, he could end up being prosecuted himself. There may be a good reason why he didn't want to disclose his part in the misconduct, but felt it was important to get the information out so that he didn't get left holding the bag. I don't know the facts, but I would suspect that he probably had some concerns."

Schwenk added, "It's hard to say why the individual did what he did, but I can certainly understand what the motivation could be. If you don't trust your commanding officer because that's who your complaint is against, you have to jump the chain and go to the next one up. And boy, when you jump from lieutenant colonel and go in to the colonel, that's a big deal in the Marine Corps, and it may not be something you want to do. You'd probably talk to people, get a sense of what their reaction is, and if you feel like you're the Lone Ranger, then you're going to mail it to somebody else, which is why we have the IG system, so there's an outside place they can go. We have independent investigative agencies, and obviously they can go to the press.

"Remember the Gold Wing hazing?" Schwenk asked. "That was the same thing. Those videotapes ended up with the media, and the media came to Marine Corps headquarters and said, 'You'll enjoy watching these videotapes,' and handed them over."

In response to the question about whether the Marine Corps would have been as forthcoming if the media had not become involved, Schwenk said, "We have allegations every day that we investigate, and we don't release a press statement on every one of them. There are hundreds and hundreds of misconduct allegations that are under investigation. The ones we do press releases on are generally important ones that really are in the public eye: murders, rapes, deaths from training accidents, or when it gets out there somehow and we're responding."

A network correspondent asked who makes the decision to release information in Article 15 (non-judicial punishment) cases, noting that sometimes information is released and other times the press is told there will be no release of details so as not to violate the Privacy Act.

A public affairs officer (PAO) replied that in the V-22 case, "the commandant of the Marine Corps decided that the charges were so important to the reputation of the corps that he chose to release the names of those charged."

The correspondent said, "That release decision seems arbitrary. A decision to release is made based on its potential value to the military institution, but release would probably be denied, invoking the Privacy Act, in a case that was potentially embarrassing to the government."

"We have allegations every day that we investigate, and we don't release a press statement on every one of them. The ones we do press releases on are generally important ones that really are in the public eye."

A retired DOD official agreed: "The act is frequently invoked in a self-serving manner. In general, the more sensitive the issue being investigated, the more people will be involved in a decision to release or withhold release of such information."

A newspaper reporter complained about the lack of ready access to basic information, such as dockets, suggesting that a list be e-mailed to the press. "All we need is the names. With military attorneys, just initials will do. A little neon light will go off if it's Gittins," he said.

A senior DOD official agreed that service-wide dockets should be available.

A magazine reporter noted that reporters approach stories of weapons and equipment investigations with skepticism because of past experience of being misled, giving problems with the Osprey as an example.

Participants noted numerous reasons why officers would want to keep quiet about problems with a service's weapons systems. Some may be key to a service's future. Others may not be essential to a service, but may be essential to an officer's future in the military, and to his life after the military, because he's going to work for Boeing or Lockheed.

"What the military has to understand is that it has a dispensation to act in a certain way," one conferee pointed out. "A commander has an authority that doesn't exist in any other subculture. Typically, the press doesn't investigate its own criminal conduct; the military does. Undue command influence is built in. It's a unique system, and it needs outside scrutiny."

In response, Schwenk said, "For all the services, the Kelly Flinn case created a big change in balancing fair trial, etcetera, with putting the word out to the American public through the media.

"The Marine Corps in particular went far out. When the commandant decided in the Cavalese case that we were going to put a guy on *60 Minutes* before the trial, that was taking the military justice system and dangling it by a thin thread on what this idiot was going to say or not say. I was the idiot. And yet the commandant said, 'That's the way we're going to do it. Don't screw up. Bye.' There's been a big change."

An Air Force participant pointed out that in the Flinn case, "the issue was lying, not adultery," but that the Air Force's hands were tied by the fact that "for purely political reasons, the general counsel of the Air Force decided not to open Article 32. We couldn't even tell people what the charges were, though they were of public record.

"We had always wanted to protect the individual, as in the Flinn case, but we will not sacrifice the institution ever again," he said. "Flinn is a landmark case; now the standard rule is to open Article 32."

A retired Army officer said, "Sometimes the media focus on the wrong issue. In the Aberdeen case, the overriding issue was not sex but command authority: if you can't trust field officers to be in control of men, how can you trust them to be in command? In the case of Kelly Flinn, if you can't trust her to tell the truth, how can you trust her to fly a B-52? The press blew it; they missed the big story."

A broadcast journalist pointed out that the public and the media are largely ignorant of the Uniform Code of Military Justice. She said, "The perception among civilians is that the system is designed to convict. The challenge is explaining that while the rules are different, they are not inherently unfair."

A magazine reporter noted that terms like military intelligence, military music and military justice are sometimes jokingly referred to as oxymorons. He asked, "Is that reputation warranted? Does the military justice system work effectively over time, or is it a charade that requires vigilance by the press to make it work?"

Gittins responded, "From my point of view, it mostly works. And that's because military officers who are doing their jobs generally try to do their duty, particularly members of court martial panels. They believe what they're doing is important and that they need to be fair in the process.

"The problem that arises is when there are external pressures on the system," he said. "The cable car case comes to mind, because there was a lot of international outcry. The case of the *Greeneville* was a problem because of relations between the Japanese and the United States and our position in the Far East; the McKinney case, because it came after Tailhook and the gender integration issues and sexual harassment issues. There's the potential that people who want to do the right thing, and believe they're doing the right thing, will try for good reasons to move things in the direction they think they should go. But as soon as you apply expedience to military justice, you've broken the system."

While agreeing that it is important for the press to exercise oversight, Gittins pointed out that the media missed what he said was an important point in the Naval Academy case: "Military members, midshipmen, had their rights *trampled*, as a matter of policy, by DOD investigators. They made a policy decision that they were going to abrogate the rights of those young men and women. That is an important story. That should have been covered, but it wasn't. It got a line or two, but nobody really cared about it. We lost in federal court, but I will tell you that almost every procedure we challenged was changed as a result of our lawsuit. So, yes, there's a place for the press, and it's in oversight."

Suessmann noted that in evaluating the credibility of an investigation, reporters should ask four questions:

• Who's directing the effort?

• Is the investigation being conducted in a manner that will allow for later judicial use? For example, are those questioned being read their rights?

• Is the investigation *unnecessarily* being conducted in a criminal context? What parameters—such as budget ceilings or number of investigators—are being placed on the investigation?

• Will the investigation results be transparent in the end?

Fargo said, "In the main, the military justice system works very well. What you don't see are the literally hundreds of cases we deal with every day that very clearly do protect good order and discipline. Every commander is familiar with the military justice system, and they take their responsibilities tremendously seriously, because it is part of the oath we took to support and defend the Constitution.

"There are issues that do come up, and one of them is the one Charlie mentioned earlier, where there is a competing interest. There's only so much capacity in the military justice system," he said.

"My initial instinct when Scott Waddle requested a particular attorney was, 'Give it to him, and get on with it,'" Fargo said. "But the more time I spent with this particular issue and talking to the

Judge Advocate General [JAG], I realized you can set a precedent that will bring the military to all-stop. If I give Scott Waddle his by-name call lawyer outside the region, then I really have an obligation to do that for an E-2 who's in Okinawa who wants a by-name call lawyer who may be in Brunswick, N.H. You have to make some decisions to allow the system to function so that you don't bring it to all-stop and you can continue to meet the fundamental mission your particular organization has."

A newspaper journalist asked about a newspaper story quoting Fargo as saying "something to the effect of, 'Something wrong happened on board that ship, and that is ultimately the responsibility of the commanding officer.' On the one hand, I thought that put the Navy in a fairly good position in terms of assuring that as the process went forward there was going to be some responsibility given to the commanding officer. At the same time, I was very surprised you made that kind of fairly strong statement prior to the legal proceeding. How did you come to make that statement, and, Charlie, what was your reaction from a defense standpoint?"

Fargo replied, "This was not to fix culpability or to say who made what mistakes, but after 30 years of doing this, and being a submariner by trade and knowing all the procedures we have in place, the *Greeneville* situation was very clearly an accident, probably one we couldn't reproduce if we tried. But we do have procedures that are designed to avoid even *accidents* from happening. And my experience is that most things, when you look at them closely, are avoidable in some manner if everything is done properly."

He went on, "And then, as Scott Waddle very clearly defined when he stepped out and talked to the press, our tradition, our responsibility, our authority under our regulations is that the commanding officer is ultimately responsible. So I don't think that was a revelation."

Gittins responded, "Certainly, had there been a trial, Adm.

Fargo's comment would have been litigated as to whether or not there was command influence. I think Adm. Fargo is a very fair and honest man and came to the right result. But could that statement have influenced some potential members of the court martial as to what they thought Adm. Fargo wanted to be the result? The possibility is yes. So we would have litigated it.

"But he was exactly right," Gittins added. "Something was wrong, and the commanding officer is ultimately responsible for what happens on his vessel. We understood that, but accountability of command does not necessarily equate to criminal liability. Our entire point at the court of inquiry was to demonstrate that there was no criminal conduct by Scott. Yes, he was in command. An accident happened, but he should not be held criminally responsible for it."

"My mission was to go up there and show a rational, reasonable human being representing a process that was supposed to be just and result in a fair end state."

A television journalist said it appears to journalists that the military's standard operating procedure is to give out as little information as possible, even after an investigation has been completed, even when there is a freedom of information request.

She asked Schwenk whether he decided to go on *60 Minutes* because of the coverage of the Flinn case on *60 Minutes* and the Air Force's "incredibly bad performance in that case."

Schwenk replied, "I think so. Gen. Krulak was markedly affected by what happened with Kelly Flinn and some of the other cases, so when the cable car case came down the track, he decided to try to put as much information out as he could within the bounds of the system. When he knew that *60 Minutes* was going to put on a program, his options were, 'No comment from the Marine Corps,' or 'Here's a paragraph,' or send a human being. My understanding is that at the meeting all the senior advisers said, 'Put a written statement out, period.' On his own he decided to send a human being."

The television journalist persisted: "What I'm trying to get at is, what was your strategy? Did you see this as going to the court of public opinion, and did you have a specific objective?"

She continued, "Of the amazing things I've heard in this room today, I think Charlie Gittins saying, 'I don't like the press' has been one of the most amazing. It seems to me the strategy has been to make the institution the defendant, even if you're the accused. The way you handled Waddle, in terms of turning him into a human being who really did have regrets, and [Capt. Richard] Ashby, who expressed no regrets at all, the public perception was that he just sort of skated through and was not held accountable in any way. Were you there to sort of balance the program?"

"*60 Minutes* wanted a balanced program," Schwenk replied. "They wanted something from the Marine Corps to balance what they were going to put on from other people. So my mission was to go up there and show a rational, reasonable human being representing a process that was supposed to be just and result in a fair end state. We were not rushed; we took our time. There was lots of due process in there. I had a 45-minute interview, whatever the sound bites were."

Gittins interjected, "Since Kelly Flinn, Gene McKinney, the Cavalese incident, Scott Waddle, there's been an evolution in how the military handles these kinds of incidents. Scott Waddle benefited a great deal from Ashby's trial. That Ashby was not found guilty for negligent homicide was an important point. I'd have to defer to Adm. Fargo, who can't talk about his decision-making process, but I am confident that our strategy at the court of inquiry showed that it would be a problematic court martial for Scott Waddle, too. The last thing the Navy wanted was an acquittal. Given Japanese public opinion, that would have been a disaster for the Navy.

"So everybody's benefited from the line of cases, post-Tailhook," he concluded. "The Navy, Marines, Army have all learned lessons about how to assure accountability."

The journalist asked Gittins if he thought he would have gotten an acquittal for Waddle.

Gittins said he believed he would, on negligent homicide: "I think it was an intervening act of negligence that would have over-ridden Scott's error, which was an honest error."

When the journalist said, "But you just didn't want to go there?" Gittins responded, "I'm a defense attorney. The last thing I want is a trial for my client. Scott could have gone to jail for three years, actually 27 years if they charged him with nine counts of negligent homicide. The last thing I wanted to do was subject him to a court martial."

Schwenk added, "They could have added other charges that he may not have beaten, and then all of a sudden he has a general court martial conviction on stuff that should have been handled elsewhere."

Fargo said, "My concern was just the opposite. After we released the full text from the court of inquiry, 2,000 pages, I wrote a nine-page statement and gave it to the press. The greatest difficulty was getting people to read it. After we released all the information, put it on Web sites, stood up in front of the press, answered questions, I still would find pieces that were being written where people obviously hadn't read much of what we had put in the public venue. It's a lesson for us. How do you get the information out? How do you get people to pay attention to it?"

Chapter 5
Investigations: Overcoming Problems

Leading off the discussion on investigations were:

  • Moderator Jeffrey Smith, Partner with Arnold & Porter with broad service in both the executive and legislative branches, including service as General Counsel of the Senate Armed Services Committee and General Counsel for the Central Intelligence Agency;

  • James Kitfield, National Security and Foreign Affairs Correspondent for National Journal *magazine;*

  • Rear Adm. Stephen Pietropaoli, the Navy's Chief of Information;

  • Brig. Gen. Timothy Ghormley, Commanding General of the 3rd Marine Expeditionary Brigade, based in Okinawa.

L awyer Jeffrey Smith pointed out that credibility is a common theme underlying the issues that come up in the relationship between the military and the media. He said, "On the part of the military, this means a reporter, a producer, an editor who will work hard to understand the facts and get them out in a way that is fair and accurate. And on the part of the media, is the person in the military with whom I am dealing telling me the truth? Is he or she giving me only partial facts? Is he spinning this in such a way that he's trying to influence the debate? Am I being used?

"A reporter at this conference said he felt that in one instance he'd been misled deliberately," he said. "When the issue was put to a broader group, the response was, 'It's not a question of *has* it happened, it's a question of how *often* it has happened.' I found that disturbing."

Smith went on, "Investigations are particularly hard, because the military is concerned with good order and discipline and accomplishing the mission. At the same time, they are concerned with due process for the servicemen or women involved, and in making sure that the outcome is the right one from that perspective."

On the other hand, he said, "The media are concerned with getting the story. They no doubt face a drumbeat from their editors and from the public. Oftentimes the family of a victim is demanding action. The family usually begins by feeling well taken care of and being sympathetic to the military. Then they often drift into antipathy toward the military, a feeling that somehow the military has misled them and that they've not been treated fairly. On top of all that, you have the Congress, which often conducts its own investigation with regard to no rules except their own, which they make up as they go along.

"A theme that runs through this is that a tragedy has occurred. There has been an accident, somebody has died, something is wrong," Smith pointed out. "Somebody must be held accountable, and that means somebody must go to jail. I suspect the military feel they are besieged on all sides, including from the press, who are demanding to know when General So-and-So will be escorted to Leavenworth in handcuffs so they can get photographs.

"The media may be thinking, 'Why is this taking so long? These people are truly incompetent and they're covering up gross misdeeds simply to benefit their own careers or their own services.'" he said. "That can be very destructive."

An Assessment from the Media

James Kitfield, national security and foreign affairs correspondent for *National Journal*, observed that "the times when the media have their watchdog hats on, which they certainly do during investigations, are when the natural tensions between our two professions are probably at their highest. So I don't think we should expect there are any silver bullets out there that are going to cure these natural tensions and make both of us happy. The first thing we have to understand is that this relationship during investigations is going to be very tense at times, one where neither side is going to be perfectly happy with the other."

However, he added, "understanding the different roles we have at least alleviates some of the personal animus that can flare up. On the journalistic side, we have to recognize that the military justice system is different. The criminal justice system is designed to be sort of a nonpartisan way of looking at wrongdoing and assigning blame for that wrongdoing. The military system is very different. They will tell you the military justice system is designed not only to do what the criminal justice system does, but also to be a tool by which local commanders can ensure good order and discipline in their commands. As such, the military system gives enormous latitude to local commanders to decide what does get pursued and what does not, who pursues those cases, who sits in judgment of those cases. So there is a whole lot of command authority invested in that local commander. That is necessary because the military is given a very, very weighty responsibility to protect the national security.

"The flip side is for the military to realize that it's inherent in that system that undue command influence can come to bear," Kitfield pointed out. "For instance, when we investigate weapon systems programs, we've seen time and time again that whoever is in charge of the weapons program has come to identify the success of that program with the success of his or her service in a way that can cloud their judgment. We journalists come in with a skeptical mind that sometimes infuriates our military counterparts, because we see as an inherent fault in the system that you've come to believe that the success of your services is tied up with those weapon systems and you're encouraged to be almost an advocate for them in terms of your life and career. Someone who questions those systems is not a welcome sight."

"We really can't expect the military to spend all its time airing its dirty laundry to us. We also have to understand that there are built-in constraints in the military system."

He added that it is important "to understand the rules set up when investigations get raised to a higher level, e.g., when the IG [Inspector General] is asked in when a senior officer has been accused of wrongdoing, and that it's very important to obey those rules very meticulously—because if that does *not* happen, it becomes very difficult for that system to work very well. A lot of us have seen this in crash investigations or friendly-fire incidents, where you typically get a command investigating itself, and the promotions of people doing the investigating are dependent on the person they're investigating. It's very difficult for that system to investigate senior people, because so much authority is invested in the hierarchical organization of the military and with that local commander."

On the other hand, Kitfield pointed out that journalists should realize "we really can't expect the military to spend all its time airing its dirty laundry to us: 'Heads up, here's our latest foible. Don't you want to report it?' Sometimes maybe we expect that. A couple of journalists here commented, 'You didn't alert us to this problem.'

I think we have to understand, human nature being what it is, that we're not going to be constantly alerted by the military to the problems it has.

"We also have to understand that there are built-in constraints in the military system," he said. "For legal reasons, we can't expect full disclosure, and sometimes people in these investigations are going to be able to manipulate the fact that the defendants frequently can speak much more freely than the people who are in charge.

"Finally, I would like to think there is recognition out there that the system, for all its tensions and inherent pressures, tends to work," Kitfield said. "If you do this long enough, you see time and time again that events work something like this: some whistle-blower decides the Bradley fighting vehicle is a death trap, and he calls some journalist, who writes a story. Then a congressman sees a chance for publicity, so he asks the GAO [General Accounting Office] to investigate. The congressman then has a hearing in which the report is revealed. Then they call up the poor sacrificial lamb from the military, who has to do his mea culpas, and they beat him up. At the end of that system, the congressman appropriates more money to fix the problem, and the problem gets fixed. We saw that time and time again with the weapon systems that we all thought in the 1980s were turkeys, like the M-1 tank, the Bradley fighting vehicle, and the Apache helicopter. They actually turned out to work quite well. But they worked quite well because they had gone through that system, and at the end of the day whatever problems they had had been fixed. However, that's not very comfortable or reassuring to people caught in the belly of that beast while they're being beat up in front of the cameras.

"But if you take the long view, you'll see that the system actually works to make our systems better, to institute reforms that we need," he concluded. Using Tailhook as an example, Kitfield said,

"Everyone says people beat up on the Navy. Well, the Navy had a culture back then that needed to change. Tailhook helped the Navy. It's a very different Navy today than it was in the late 1980s, a better Navy. So the system works. If we keep that long view in mind, both sides will be more willing to put up with the tensions of the short term."

Why the Military Can't Speak

Rear Adm. Stephen Pietropaoli, Chief of Information for the Navy, noted that "we in the military carry around a few pat phrases like, 'neither confirm nor deny.' We don't question that. It's like the Ten Commandments that it's inappropriate to comment while the matter is under investigation or pending litigation. During the *Greeneville* investigation, as people were beating up on us about the release of names, saying, 'Look, the NTSB [National Transportation Safety Board] is standing up every day jawboning about what they found. Why can't you be more transparent?' We'd go to the index card, and it said, 'Inappropriate to comment while the matter is under investigation.'

"The fact is we're different," Pietropaoli said. "Command influence is part of that. But the fundamental difference is, we own the investigation. Particularly when it's an informal investigation, it's going to be a closed investigation. We then own the responsibility for determining how to adjudicate the findings and take corrective action, possibly disciplinary action. And, in a twist unlike anything elsewhere, we own the jury pool. So any statements we make about the investigation, as innocent as they might seem at the time, even if they are generic statements like, 'This is how a submarine periscope search is supposed to be done,' can wind up in Mr. Gittins' command influence file for the potential court martial, and are going to be read by potential jurors.

"I'm not railing about how unfair it is," he pointed out. "The government has a lot of advantages. The 'disadvantage' is that we are seriously constrained about how much it's appropriate for us to talk. When you go to a formal fact-finding body like the court of inquiry, and under Article 32 people are designated as parties and have attorneys and rights are protected, it can be much more transparent. But in an informal investigation, which is most of what we do, the system is best served, frankly, when we shut up and let the facts speak for themselves. That's very frustrating to almost every journalist in this room. It should be. You'll do your damnedest to circumvent it, and we understand that. But our people have to have confidence that the system won't be skewed by outside pressure. The public is not well served if we fall victim to the pressure to correct the record because others are willing to come forward.

"Probably the most important thing I learned in the last year was to peel back from that mantra of 'inappropriate to comment while the matter is under investigation' to determine why it is inappropriate," Pietropaoli said. "I had to go through this drill in front of the press corps at the Pentagon myself to say, 'You know, we hadn't really thought about this.' That was instructive for a lot of people in the press corps who had heard the same thing for years but hadn't really thought it through either."

The next speaker was Brig. Gen. Timothy Ghormley, commanding general of the 3rd Marine Expeditionary Brigade in Okinawa. Ghormley noted he was Inspector General of the Marine Corps during the Osprey investigation. He said more openness might have mitigated some of the bad press the Marines received.

"We could have gone a long way by explaining the readiness reporting system, exactly what was going on, and what in fact had been falsified. They weren't maintenance records; they were readiness records. But it was a readiness reporting system that inherently reported much lower numbers. Instead of trying to justify, or maybe that's the wrong word, instead of trying to make the numbers fit, we should have explained, 'This system is going to report lower automatically.' That would have eased some of the suspicion," he said.

"One of the big problems we have is when we do open up for an investigation," he said. "We have eight officers right now going up for non-judicial punishment, Article 15. The three-star that's going to hold that captain's mast has been reading all this. He's under pressure already. There's a lot of pressure out there on this commanding general to make a judgment on eight officers. What will the press response be if half those officers walk? Are you going to be able to establish credibility and keep it? I don't think so, not if we're going to keep working under the same set of rules we have right now."

Q & A: Many Issues

A newspaper reporter pointed out that there were two Osprey investigations: the legal investigation and the safety investigation. He said the safety investigation "is very close in model to the NTSB investigation, in that they're fact-finders; they're not part of a chain of command, and whatever they say or do has nothing to do with the legal side. Is that possibly an opening where you could get at least factual information out, which sometimes takes months to get?"

Pietropaoli responded, "One of the problems is that safety center investigations often are done with privilege in order to find out the cause, not to assess accountability. Frequently, rights are *not* read, and those investigations are not meant to be public. The overriding equity there is to make sure people continue to be forthcoming. They've done a very, very strong job over the years of protecting that privilege, including taking it to very high courts to protect the privilege.

"The other side is a JAG [Judge Advocate General] investigation, which is done with sworn testimony," he said. "The problem is in releasing it as you go along, not in releasing it at the end. We should do a better job, no doubt, but we've had cases in which appeals courts have decided to throw out convictions because they perceived that the institution engaged in a kind of media campaign to paint this individual as guilty of something in the way they released 'facts' during the investigative process. Whether that was indeed part of the plan or not, if that is the post-facto impression given to the appeals court, you can wind up not being able to assess accountability because of the way you handled the investigation.

"You hate to reduce it to the lowest common denominator," Pietropaoli said. "You have to weigh maintaining public confidence in the institution against the value of getting convictions, but at the end of the day, the system has to protect the due process of the individuals involved and the confidence of those sailors, soldiers, airmen, marines who have to live under the UCMJ [Uniform Code of Military Justice]. We are right to draw the line pretty far to the left in protecting the process and enduring the slings and arrows until the end of the investigation, at which time we should be probably more forthcoming than we often are."

A broadcast journalist suggested that there is a middle ground, "and that is that it benefits all of us to get the facts straight. If we don't get the facts straight it damages not only *our* credibility, but the credibility of the service of the people involved."

Returning to the *Greeneville* investigation, the journalist said, "I'm perfectly willing to take information on background or even deep background. And when I talk to Steve [Pietropaoli] or one of his people, they can say to me, which they did, 'Here are some of the issues that are being discussed and looked into: should he have done a second periscope sweep? Should he have tried this emergency ascent nine miles off Diamondhead?'

"Give me some of the issues to talk about," he urged. "'Here are the options as far as the legal procedures are concerned. We can do A, B, C or D.' And then say, 'Look, we can't talk because the investigation is under way, but here are a couple of people, retired submariners, you can call. Here are their telephone numbers.' Of course, you pick them out ahead of time, knowing they are lucid and know what they're doing. But instead of getting the official Navy line, we call them and we get the *facts*. So we come up with a decent story. It's so much better than stonewalling and saying, 'Cannot discuss it because it's under investigation.'"

There's a big difference between asking a retired officer for general procedural information and asking him for opinions on the specific case.

An Army general demurred: "If the military were to give you the names of some talking heads, would they be credible? Or would you say, 'Well, they have to say that because that's the party line'? I think you all have your own sources of talking heads out there and you'll go out and get them anyway, whether they're briefed or not."

The journalist replied, "Knowing you and your credibility, and having worked with you, if you said to me, 'Why don't you talk to Col. So-and-So or Gen. So-and-So,' I know damn well that that's going to be a good guy or gal I can talk to and get facts from. And I can tell very quickly in my conversation with that person whether or not that's true. But it gives me a definite lead, which serves your cause and also serves mine. It's just an added ability to try and get the facts so we can do something that's honest and fair."

Pietropaoli said such sources can be useful: "The reason we sometimes use proxies (retired individuals who are knowledgeable about procedures) is because if a retired individual goes through what the routine periscope sweep is, that's one thing. If a sitting naval officer, someone senior in the chain of command to be credible, or a commanding officer does it, it could go in that command influence file."

But Pietropaoli cautioned that there's a big difference between asking a retired officer for general procedural information about how things work and asking him for opinions on the specific case or investigation.

"An awful lot of people are probably not going to know the facts [of the case], and I'm sure not going to tell them whatever I think are facts to help them unless they're out there in public domain and they just don't have them. We've just got to be very careful about that. On the facts of what the investigation is finding, I won't tell you, 'Here's a guy outside the service you can go to for the facts,' because the chances are, they'll have worse facts than I have."

Another journalist expanded on the limits of using retired officers as sources: "The media too often think they can get any retired general, or admiral, or other person to comment on anything within the military, and so you'll have people commenting outside their expertise range. It's helpful if someone can steer a media person toward someone who has had experience with that kind of thing, not just the military in general. But far too often we see people quoted about things that weren't in their own experience or about something that's changed significantly since they were there."

A lawyer said, "On the issue of background, deep background, and command influence, defense lawyers, like reporters, are not stupid." He said if he sees a story referring to an unnamed Pentagon spokesman, he tries to figure out who it is. "Then, I'm going to call him to an Article 32 [investigation] and put him under oath and say, 'Sir, did you say that?' I have to trust that a naval officer is going to tell the truth when asked that direct question. If he's going to have the integrity to tell the truth, then we've got our command influence; I've proved it right there. That's why you very rarely see commanders making those kinds of statements in investigations."

A senior Army officer noted that "in the court of public opinion, military investigations are not conducted on a level playing field. Defense attorneys have the opportunity to speak publicly if it suits their cause; prosecutors are often muted by the concern of implying command influence or because of pretrial agreements."

He added that when a gay soldier was beaten to death at Ft. Campbell, Ky., "junior officers on base felt their commanding general 'did everything right' in handling the investigations and punishments, but felt the Army hung the general out to dry to show that the institution was dealing with the issue seriously. Junior officers took this as a lesson that they were expendable individually to achieve a political goal, even if their actions stood up to legal scrutiny."

Kitfield asked when, if ever, military people think it's OK to mislead the media and when media people think they've been misled. He noted that "what really gets the media's goat is when they feel they're being misled. I don't think it happens very often, but I can think of a few incidents."

In particular, he cited questions regarding use of Apache helicopters during Kosovo, "because we were all told that the problems in using the Apaches were because of the logistics problem, with three feet of mud. That's why the big delay. But Wes Clark's book would suggest something very dramatically different was happening. We were being misled there, I think. Is it ever OK to mislead us?" he asked.

Gen. Dennis Reimer went on the record to say, "There is a complex issue in terms of the [Apache] deployment, and the Army took a heavy hit. If you go back and look at Goldwater-Nichols, you'll find that the person responsible for the deployment of the use of his assets is the Commander-in-Chief. Those helicopters belong to

SACEUR [Supreme Allied Commander, Europe] and CINCEUR [Commander-in-Chief, Europe], and the assets available were being stretched for humanitarian reasons. The priorities he [Gen. Wesley Clark] established at that time were absolutely correct. The decision to deploy Task Force Hawk was a two-part decision. One was a deployment decision and the second was to be an employment decision. So the slowness of the Apaches could have been accelerated if we'd put the priority on putting the assets there to get them there.

"It is true, we went into the worst place I've ever seen," he said. "That was a mud hole and those soldiers did an absolutely wonderful job. If you don't believe me, go talk to Forrest Sawyer, who was over there with the *Nightline* crew. Forrest came back to me and really grilled me hard on why I didn't let them be employed.

"The second part of that decision was, do you need to employ them?" Reimer recalled. "I went over there toward the end of my tour, mid-May. I looked every one of those commanders in the eye and made an assessment myself of whether I thought they were ready. My conclusion was that they were ready.

"The issue then becomes a risk/benefit analysis," he said. "At that time, the weather had started to clear, the Air Force was able to get better targeting data; the Air Force commanders on the ground told me they could do the job without the Apaches. There were only about two or three entry points into Kosovo from Albania; the Apaches had to go through those passes. It was a high-risk operation, and my advice at that time was that if the risk is worth it, the Apaches are ready to do their job. I think that's what the commanders on the ground felt, too. But by that time things were going a lot better for us from the air standpoint on targets in Kosovo, and I think the conclusion for most of us was that it really wasn't worth the risk at that point in time."

Kitfield asked again if that meant that in time of war there are occasions when it is OK to mislead the press.

Reimer responded, "Is there a time to mislead? My opinion? In peacetime, absolutely not. In wartime, there may be some issues of national security that might warrant a decision like that, but that ought to be carefully thought through."

A Pentagon spokesman commented, "You all do a good enough job of sometimes misleading yourselves in wartime. Take a look at the 'amphibious landing' during Desert Storm. That was completely drummed up by the media themselves. Somebody was just graceful enough to throw an exercise and let the media cover it. All of a sudden it became an amphibious landing, which was by all definition a deception, yet no official spokesman ever told a media member that we were going to conduct an amphibious landing. They always said, 'We have the capability to do that, and we'll make the decision at the right time,' which is true. So there's probably not a lot of need to mislead anybody during wartime."

A print journalist expressed surprise at what Reimer had said about the Apaches: "Gen. Cody's memo that came on after the war saying these guys were not ready to fight when they got there was in direct contrast to what we were told in a Pentagon briefing by the Army's Apache program manager, that this was the best-trained Apache unit in the Army. Can you square that?"

Reimer replied, "Those Apaches had just come out of Grafenwoehr, Germany and had gone through rotation, so the feeling was that they were ready. You have to understand that the flying conditions in Germany are much different than in Albania, and the fact that we were going to use the Apaches with a targeting system that was located in Macedonia—we didn't have anybody on the ground to give us the targeting data—caused us some really significant issues in terms of putting that package together.

"So yes, they were trained individually, but being synchronized with the UAVs [unmanned aerial vehicles] flying out of Macedonia, with an MLRS [multiple launch rocket system] system that's out of

Albania—that had to be done," he said. "And we had to get used to the high-altitude flying, the flying at night. We lost a couple of birds. We lost a couple of outstanding troops. All of that had to be done, and we knew it would take us awhile to do that when we deployed them, so we wanted to get them over there so that if we needed them we could use them. Again, at the time that they were ready to go as a synchronized package, our feeling was that the risk didn't justify the benefit."

When it comes to lying, a broadcast journalist said, "Very few people have deliberately lied to me. Usually, it's a matter of omitting key facts, steering away, because they know the reporter is going to come back. There's going to be an unpleasant confrontation down the road. And we become highly skeptical."

A government spokesman added, "If you mislead a journalist, you're done. That's not to say that you have to automatically provide every bit of information. There have been many cases where I've known the answer to a question, but until you ask just the right question, I'm not going to give you that answer. And then if you were to ask the right question, I'd probably say, 'I can't answer that.' Many journalists have then said, 'Can you not answer that because you don't know the answer or because you can't tell me?' That's a fair question to ask and a fair question to answer."

He went on, "If we got to a point where to go further would be to jeopardize something, then you're faced with a situation of saying 'I can't tell you more, but you have to weigh that against, were you to write a story that pointed in this direction, you would be wrong. I'm not going to help steer you where you would be right, but you would put someone in jeopardy.' Do we have to tell the media everything? No. Is it better if you try to warn the journalist off moving in a certain direction? Actually, yes. That would be useful, depending on the circumstance."

A broadcast journalist contrasted the Flinn case, which was

closed, and the McKinney case, which was open: "Is there any winner either way?" she asked. "Even though the McKinney case was open, it seemed like the Army took as many hits [as the Air Force had with the Flinn case]. By the end of the case, here was a guy who was accused of all these egregious things by women who didn't know each other and were sort of separated geographically, yet they weren't able to come up with a conviction. On one side you weren't able to get the facts out and on the other side you were, but it seemed like it was a loser both ways."

"There are three ways to answer any question: 'I know and I can tell you;' 'I know but I can't tell you;' and 'I don't know.' If you stick with those three, you're probably going to be all right."

A lawyer said, "From my point of view, the Air Force shot themselves in the foot in the Flinn case. That should have been an open hearing. At that stage in an Article 32 [investigation] transparency is good. Sunshine disinfects, and you can have confidence that the process is working."

He theorized that having an open, transparent and thorough Article 32 investigation was critical in the McKinney case because it enabled every fact relevant to the accusations to emerge, with the whole thing transcribed verbatim.

However, the lawyer noted, "Nobody wins in a court martial. Even if Gene McKinney had been completely acquitted, he's not vindicated. His reputation's been damaged. The Army took some hits; the investigators took some hits; certainly the alleged victims took hits. Nobody was a winner in that process."

An Army general noted that one reason the Army would have preferred that the McKinney hearing be closed was to protect the witnesses. The reporter pointed out that the Flinn and McKinney cases were both "of a sexual nature. There was some pretty rough stuff that went on during the McKinney investigation. If a woman is accusing a man and she knows that she's going to be out in public, what effect does that have?"

The general replied that that was his concern, also: "That's why we would have preferred to keep it closed, because there were probably some innocent women who got trashed there."

Pietropaoli summed up the case for honesty: "I just would remind all the operators in the room that as the Navy spokesperson, I'm expendable. They can go out and replace me tomorrow. But I'm not speaking for Steve Pietropaoli. It's not my integrity that's on the line when I speak; it's the Secretary of the Navy's and the chief of naval operations. You can't throw your spokesman out there and let him mislead. You can do that if you want to do it once, but the next spokesman you send out will not be at all helpful to you. The one you just destroyed is in the trash bin; the next one is immediately suspect.

"So my recommendation for operators and PAOs alike is Dan Rather's advice on how to answer any question," he said. "There are three ways to answer any question: 'I know and I can tell you;' 'I know but I can't tell you;' and 'I don't know.' If you stick with those three, you're probably going to be all right."

He noted that there will be times when reporters have information that could put an operation in jeopardy. He cited an instance in which Fred Francis of NBC agreed to delay reporting a story about carriers heading for Libya.

"Did NBC get any advantage out of their forbearance? Yes. They had the reporter in Tripoli open a phone line and keep it open, so that when everybody else couldn't get a phone line, NBC had one. And they probably had better information on exactly what we were doing because they were responsible in withholding the information until after the pilots were safely outbound.

"But by and large, we're getting too cute," Pietropaoli concluded. "We're not good at doing cute nuance in the military. We're better sticking with *'I know,'* *'I don't know,'* or *'I can't tell you.'* "

Chapter 6
Conference Conclusions

The irregular triangle formed by the military, the media, and civilian leadership so eloquently described by Andrew Bacevich lay at the heart of much of the discussion that took place during the McCormick Tribune Foundation's sixth military-media conference. Though differing points of view were expressed by representatives of the military and the media, they were largely united in their frustration with the Bush administration.

The overriding issue that emerged was *communication*—between the military and the media and from the civilian leadership to both the military and the media. As one military participant put it, "A consistent theme [of the conference] has been that this administration or this agency is not doing a good job of communicating the message. I always twinge when I hear that…But what we've seen in the first eight months here is you've got to have the message first. They [the Bush administration] have been in message formation for the last eight months."

A broadcaster noted that although reporting on the Quadrennial Defense Review (QDR) on television was like "trying to shape a cloud, people do want to know what's going on…We're all trying to make sure that the way we report it and the way you shape it is really taking us to face the right things out there in a very complex and difficult world, as attacks on the *USS Cole* and other terrorist attacks have shown us. We're not in the same camp, but we are kind of in this together. And if we can ever figure out what the strategy is, we'll try to communicate it," she concluded.

Participants expressed frustration at the absence of representatives from the Bush administration. A newspaper editor said if administration representatives had attended, "we, of course, would all have asked, 'Without a White House national security strategy, how can the Pentagon write its national military strategy? Without a national military strategy, how deep, how definite can the QDR actually be? How smart can the budgets be?'"

Referring to a line from a country and western song, "If you don't know where you're going, any road will do," he said, "That's how those of us covering the Pentagon today feel about this administration's national security strategy."

He went on, "The Bush White House political appointees came in hating the press. There's nothing wrong with that. There are days when I hate the press. The Clinton administration no doubt hated the press as well. But at least the Clintonites understood the famous Vladimir Lenin dictum about using the press as useful idiots. I don't think we're idiots, but I know that we're very, very useful, and to ignore us is a big mistake.

"The bottom line," he said "is the trust and the credibility that's come up many, many times, and that's why these meetings are so crucial. You break bread, you knock back a few beers, and you do realize that we are people.

"Most of the military members I've talked to who really hate the press had a very bad experience early in their career, perhaps as captains or majors, maybe even after they got their first stars. That's too bad," he added. "Yes, we have different agendas; yes, we disagree. But I hope that experiences like this can start a healing process as you get to know us as individuals and understand what our job really is.

"What we do is tell stories. We're always looking for the smartest, most compelling narrative. Unless you offer your narrative to us, I guarantee we will choose another. If you offer to share a narrative, I'm not going to promise we're going to tell the story your way, but at least you have a chance. If you don't give us that opportunity, my guarantee is we will tell another story, probably one you don't like," he concluded.

Another journalist suggested that "maybe journalists in general are failing. We tend not to give our readers some of the history as often as we should. We need to really try a little bit harder so our readers understand that the reason we're telling them something now is because, for example, back in February they said 'top-down,' but now they're saying 'no, that's not the case.' We need to remind the readers of that, because, frankly, they're just like us; they have short-term memory problems, too.

"I think also that the military does not do anything very fast except for fighting a war," he said. "When it comes to policy, buying weapons, transforming itself, it can't turn on a dime. And when the military *does* do it, we have a lot of fun writing about it because, like any organization that tries to turn too fast one way or another, mistakes are made, problems happen, and of course that's our lifeblood.

"But we haven't really made the picture clear to readers when we're talking about QDR and strategy that anything the military does, like buying strategic missile defense or anything other than black berets, takes them five to 10 years," he said. "When they make a policy change, it takes five or 10 years, which is one, or two, or three administrations later. So stuff that Bush One did back in 1992 is coming to fruition today. Stuff Clinton did in 1996, a lot of that is going to happen tomorrow. Stuff that Bush Two does, some of the people in this room are going to be dead when that comes to fruition. I hate to criticize ourselves, but sometimes I think we need to do more to explain that to readers. Maybe we haven't done as good a job as we could, and of course we never will, but we should try."

Moderator Jeffrey Smith brought the conference to a close

and set the stage for the next one by saying, "The United States is the only country in the world formed with an idea. We're held together by an idea, the idea enshrined in the Constitution, the Bill of Rights, that we're all created equal, we're held together by the rule of law. The success of that idea, in turn, depends very much on what U.S. servicemen and women are doing at the end of a pointed spear, which in turn evolves very much from the national strategy, which evolves from the debate we have been discussing here. It is hard to overstate the importance of what goes on in the military-media exchange to the future of the nation, of maintaining the idea that the founding fathers gave us.

"It is important never to lose sight of the fact that in the tension over the *Greeneville*, or Kelly Flinn, or the QDR, what's really going on here is democracy," Smith concluded. "And each side has an enormously important role to play to develop this idea as it continues to mature."

Chapter 7
The Relationship After Sept. 11:
An Administration View

The Cantigny conference occurred in the month before America's world changed with the destruction of the World Trade Center and the attack on the Pentagon. To update the dialogue begun at the conference to encompass developments since Sept. 11, 2001, the Foundation asked three people—one from each point of Bacevich's "irregular triangle" of civilian leadership, media and military—to comment on the nature of the relationship since Sept. 11.

The following article, representing the point of view of the Bush administration, is by Victoria Clarke, Assistant Secretary of Defense for Public Affairs.

The Department of Defense (DOD) believes informing the public is more than our obligation. Our charter, the Principles of Information, states, "It is Department of Defense policy to make available timely and accurate information so that the public, the Congress, and the news media may assess and understand the facts about national security and defense strategy." In the war on terrorism, that obligation has also become an imperative for victory as well. The public's understanding and support lay the very foundation of our success.

This is true for several reasons. The nature of the threat itself requires an alert, vigilant public. The war, like the threat, is unconventional. Rather than fighting the clearly identifiable military of a clearly identifiable nation, our enemies are terrorist regimes and secret cells dispersed across the world. Consequently, we must think and act differently—and the best ideas are the product of transparent government and rigorous public discussion.

The military and the media, an unlikely team, feed their needs from each other. The military needs the media as a conduit of information to the public; the media use the military in their efforts to fulfill the needs of their sponsors and audiences.

The stark contrast in the military-media relationship is the presence of competition. The military is driven by operational necessity rather than a 24-hour news cycle. The media, on the other hand, are constantly working to be the first to break a story. Each recognizes that first reports are often incorrect or incomplete. This was proven a correct adage during the months following Sept. 11, for both military information and media reporting.

Prior to the Gulf War, the media worked generally on more traditional deadlines and had more time to develop their stories. Today, they are faced with a highly competitive market that now reports around the clock. While this adds more pressure to produce more news, it also allows the luxury of being able to update its story on a continuing basis. They can beat their competitors simply by being the first to mention an event and then can develop the details as they become available. Speed often overcomes accuracy in getting a story to the public.

In a recent book written by Stanislav Lunev, a former Russian spy, he states that he was amazed at how many times he found sensitive information in the newspaper. In his view, American newspapers tend to care more about scooping their competition than about national security. DOD continues to face the challenge of balancing the needs of security with the right of the public to know. In nearly all instances, the media recognize the need to protect national security and the safety of our service members and will not publish information that will be harmful. This highlights the importance of the media working closely with DOD to ensure information is not prematurely disclosed.

The military, with an appetite to verify information, often does not meet established deadlines for responding to queries from the media. This is not voluntary reluctance but cautious hesitance to ensure the release of accurate information in the timeliest manner.

The military and the media share the requirement of carefully balancing the release of timely and accurate information. The military requires information to filter through appropriate command channels, and investigations to be completed as necessary followed by the release of the facts relative to a situation. The media's tasks are similar. Information is received through established sources, military and others. Once armed with initial information, they must then decide what to cross check and how to determine the validity of the information, not just from a single source, but also from each side of an issue.

In each of these two sets of responsibilities there is room for improvement.

The fact that the war is unconventional also makes the transformation of the military, a process that was already under way before Sept. 11, all the more important. Transformation includes much more than new weapons systems. It encompasses all the changes and adjustments in the way we train, fight and equip our forces. It also addresses the leadership necessary and the way our armed forces are integrated with their civilian counterparts. As one of the elements of national power, the American public has the right and the need to know how its military is organized and will be employed.

Finally, Americans should be informed because our nation should know, and take pride in, what we have already achieved.

Just a year ago, Afghanistan was an outlaw state and a training ground for terrorists. Its people were brutally repressed. A harsh winter threatened them with mass starvation.

Today, the people of Afghanistan are liberated, and a transitional government is paving the way for freedom and hope. The terrorist network that was poisoning their country has been debilitated. The widely forecasted humanitarian catastrophe was averted after the United States and our allies intervened, dropping 500,000 metric tons of food, enough for nearly 7 million hungry people.

Working with our allies, we've rounded up some 600 terrorist suspects in Afghanistan and hundreds more around the globe. The intelligence they are providing is saving lives by giving us the information we need to defend against future attacks. And a total of some 70 nations are now allied in the global war against terror.

It bears repeating that the United States and our partners around the world have a long way to go in the war on terror. But the ground we have yet to cover should not obscure our view of the substantial distance we have already come.

That is a fitting description of the military's relationship with the media as well.

In discussing the war on terrorism, Defense Secretary Donald Rumsfeld has said the military is learning all the time. That is certainly an apt characterization of DOD's often successful but occasionally errant efforts to keep the American people informed about the first war of the 21st century.

The media and military alike are navigating new terrain, from the proliferation of news outlets to new circumstances on the battlefield to the instantaneous dissemination of information. By and large, each institution is meeting the other's needs. Usually, DOD complies with journalists' requests for information and access. Most of the time, journalists respect the Department's need to safeguard certain information that could place operations or troops at risk.

But that is not always the case, nor is that always a problem. The most important lesson of this chapter in the military-media relationship may be this: a certain amount of tension between the two reflects the health of, not a weakness in, our democracy.

The Constitution guarantees freedom of the press while also requiring government to provide for the common defense. The McCormick Tribune Foundation understands the occasional tension between those goals. Its namesake, Col. Robert R. McCormick, was often torn between them.

He began his colorful professional life as a soldier and finished it as the publisher of the *Chicago Tribune*. McCormick's long-running feud with President Franklin Roosevelt reached a bitter peak—or nadir, depending on one's perspective—over the *Tribune's* coverage of World War II.

The McCormick-FDR rivalry was not, to be sure, always a healthy one. The *Tribune's* printing of classified war plans as well as its published revelation that the United States had broken Japanese naval codes arguably placed both the war effort and the lives of servicemen at risk—both circumstances that echo the firm line DOD has taken against leaks of classified information in the war on terror.

But for the most part, what tension exists between the media and military, then as now, results from each responsibly playing its respective role in a free society: the media reporting as much news as possible, and the military protecting operational success and the safety of troops.

The extent of media access that DOD has facilitated to the war on terrorism is proof that, more often than not, those are compatible objectives.

On the night Operation Enduring Freedom was launched, 39 journalists from 26 news organizations around the world were aboard deployed Naval vessels. A hundred journalists were on the flight line to cover C-17 aircrews returning from the first drops of humanitarian rations over Afghanistan. The Department also conducted training for journalists to prepare them for high-altitude flights in order to open an avenue of coverage for the humanitarian airdrop missions. DOD has facilitated more than 1,400 embeds [reporters allowed to live with military units] with deployed troops as well, including access to Special Forces in the field.

In addition to facilitating media embeds, DOD continually sought to expand the number of products available to the media through internal means. In October, the day following the first ground action of the campaign, Joint Combat Camera Center footage of a special operations mission was released. Coverage of the preparation and execution of a mission was made public within hours of the operation. This demonstrated that while media may be periodically restricted from covering an event for security reasons, DOD assets can be used to provide real-time coverage to the world.

Another practice, which had its beginnings in the Gulf War, is the transmission of gun camera footage to relay the effects of the ongoing air campaign. Once again this is an example of DOD providing information where access by the media is hindered either for security or space reasons. These resources allow for the classified actions of the Department to be filmed in real time for release following the completion of a sensitive operation.

All told, DOD has responded to more than 42,000 media inquiries, hosted more than 5,000 media visits to military facilities, given more than 1,500 interviews and conducted more than 225 press briefings since Sept. 11.

Journalists have also been given unprecedented access to top DOD officials. Secretary Rumsfeld has held more than 100 press briefings and availabilities (many of them with Gen. Richard Myers, Chairman of the Joint Chiefs) as well as more than 70 interviews. Gen. Tommy Franks, the operation commander, has held media briefings at the Pentagon and via video-teleconference from his headquarters in Florida. The Office of the Assistant Secretary of Defense for Public Affairs has maintained a regular dialogue with bureau chiefs and other journalists as well.

That is not to say our record has been perfect. Far from it: on some occasions, our judgment was off; on others, the information we provided was wrong.

In the chaos following a friendly-fire incident near Kandahar in which 24 U.S. and anti-Taliban soldiers were killed or wounded, troops on the scene initially denied journalists access to the casualties. The journalists were incensed, and they were right. We apologized and, more importantly, put more public affairs personnel on the ground and clarified procedures to prevent another misunderstanding.

On another occasion, the Pentagon announced that a GPS device discovered in Afghanistan appeared to have belonged to an Army Ranger who was killed in action in Somalia, strongly suggesting a connection between Al Qaeda and Somali warlords. We believed that information was accurate when we released it. But it wasn't, which journalists reported when they compared the make and model of the device with those used by the Rangers in Somalia. We corrected the information as soon as we confirmed it was wrong.

Those incidents illustrate one new dynamic of warfighting and war reporting in the Information Age: we can be quick, or we can be accurate, but is a challenge to be both at the same time. With news hitting the airwaves or Internet almost as quickly as it happens, journalists are understandably impatient for information. Our challenge is to find a balance between speed and precision—being as quick as we can and as accurate as possible. And, perhaps most important, the confusion of the battlefield produces errors under the best of circumstances, let alone the most challenging, so we must be willing to correct mistakes as soon as possible after we make them.

The military and media alike are also learning that we must be flexible and adaptable. This war is unlike any we have ever fought, so it is also unlike any for which we have ever facilitated coverage.

Before Operation Enduring Freedom, most decisions about access to deployed troops were governed by previously determined regulations. In the war on terror, the military and media, like the warfighters, have learned to improvise, such as by creating smaller, regional media pools to reflect smaller, nimbler fighting units.

These circumstances—facilitating access, correcting mistakes and adapting to new circumstances—cover the vast majority of interactions between the military and media. Even decisions not to share information often involve circumstances, such as the safety of troops, on which each institution generally agrees.

Conflicts arise, as they always do, amid shades of gray. With the lives of men and women in uniform in the balance, DOD errs, perhaps too often, on the side of caution. With their responsibility to pursue the news on the line, journalists push, perhaps too aggressively on occasion, for more access than DOD thinks it is safe to give them.

Who stands to lose the most from altering their current practices? A mistake by the media in reporting information quickly, before the facts are fully known, is fixed by a correction run in the paper or an on-the-air adjustment to the facts. A mistake by the military in releasing information prematurely can result in the loss of lives and jeopardize national security, neither of which can be fixed by running a correction.

Our challenge is to find the balance of tension between the military and the media that benefits a free society yet still facilitates the flow of information to the public. A knowledgeable, aware citizenry is too important to the war on terrorism for either institution to accept anything less.

Chapter 8
The Relationship After Sept. 11:
A Media View

Jamie McIntyre, senior Pentagon correspondent for Cable News Network (CNN), wrote this article outlining the media's view of information management since Sept. 11. He has covered military affairs for CNN since November 1992.

J ust so there is no misunderstanding, I should say at the outset that the U.S. military and the American media remain at loggerheads over the proper way to cover a war.

Of the many examples of how differently the press and the Pentagon see the world, perhaps one of the most illustrative came early on in the Afghanistan war, at a Pentagon briefing Saturday, Oct. 20, 2001, the morning after the first major U.S. ground operation.

U.S. Army Rangers and Special Forces had gone into Afghanistan the night before to gather intelligence at the compound of Taliban leader Mullah Mohamed Omar, and to check out an abandoned airstrip to see if it would be suitable for a forward operating base. That airstrip would later become Camp Rhino.

The workers at the Office of the Assistant Secretary of Defense for Public Affairs were feeling quite proud of themselves that next morning. After some hard work overnight, they had pulled off a notable first. Along with the standard briefing slides, there would also be released a short highlight reel showing actual footage from the operation the night before.

The pictures narrated by the new Joint Chiefs Chairman, Gen. Richard Myers, included infrared white-and-black images of Army paratroopers dropping from C-130s as well as eerie green night-vision video of U.S. troops on the ground poking around some abandoned buildings.

The Pentagon's Public Affairs Chief, Assistant Secretary of Defense Victoria Clarke, was still gushing over the achievement when she met with network bureau chiefs a few days later.

"I think a lot of your correspondents appreciated that," Clarke told the media executives gathered in her office. "If you had been in the briefing room when they saw that stuff, and I heard guys who have been in this business for 20 or 30 years say that's amazing."

CNN did appreciate it. It certainly made illustrating CNN's report that Saturday morning much easier. Instead of the usual map graphics and file pictures, it had actual from-the-scene images to accompany the story—enough for a two-minute television report, with nothing of significance to spare.

But while the Pentagon PR staff was puffing out its chest, many veteran reporters remained troubled by the idea that their entire understanding of the operation came from the top general at the Pentagon and a heavily edited (censored might not be too strong a word) videotape, which they were being asked to accept at face value.

I expressed those reservations in my live report, which immediately followed the briefing. I knew well from my decade of covering the Pentagon that first reports are always incomplete and often wrong, that accounts from four-stars at the Pentagon far from the battle rarely match the accounts from the ground, and that military commanders have a natural inclination to put the best face on even a disastrous mission.

For example, in Somalia in 1993 when U.S. special forces

mistakenly rounded up United Nations workers instead of warlords, a Pentagon spokesman told me with a straight face that the mission was a success, but the intelligence had been wrong, the military version of the "the operation was a success but the patient died."

The press's exclusion from covering the mission was a sore point that was pressed by CNN's Bob Franken at a contentious Pentagon briefing the following Monday. Why, Franken wanted to know, was the coverage, in his words, "controlled absolutely by the military and the government?" And shouldn't the press be allowed to parachute in with the troops?

Secretary of Defense Donald Rumsfeld seemed dumbfounded. "I'm amazed at the question," he said. After a pause, he explained, "I would think that the world would fully understand that it does not make sense, when a handful of American soldiers are parachuting into a hostile place and are going to be fully occupied in dealing with the opposition forces and shooting them, to the extent it's necessary, collecting intelligence, photographing things so that they know what's going on, and then being extracted—the idea of embedding a press pool into that group seems to me to be outside of the realm of reasonableness."

That exchange was ridiculed in a political cartoon in the *Richmond Times-Dispatch*, depicting a big-bellied Pentagon reporter whining "Why can't reporters tag along on special operations missions in Afghanistan?"

While Bob Franken would vigorously dispute the suggestion he is either unwilling or unable to jump out of an airplane in pursuit of unfiltered news from the warfront, the cartoon captured the prevailing Zeitgeist, namely that when it came to keeping the news media in the dark, American public opinion appeared to be squarely in the Pentagon's corner.

Pentagon briefings were "must-see TV" in October 2001. The war was still fresh, and fraught with uncertainty, and its leader, 69-

year-old Donald Rumsfeld had turned out to be a surprisingly charismatic Secretary of War.

Even as Rumsfeld was still lecturing the assembled press corps that October day, e-mails from the viewing public began to pop into the inbox of the Pentagon's Directorate for Public Inquiry and Analysis. Of the 70 or so e-mail messages and calls received that day, all but two took the side of Rumsfeld and the Defense Department.

Here's a sample:

"I have no idea the name of the reporter who could not understand why he could not jump in with the Rangers. I had no idea that you allowed first graders to ask questions." (Descano, Calif.)

"Your performance in the face of the press' inane questions and their attitudes of self-centered conceit that somehow THEY protect American interests is masterful, and a joy to watch." (Indianapolis, Ind.)

"They don't get it. This is not a football game requiring play by play." (Palm Beach Shores, Fla.)

"We applaud the fact that you give as little information as possible to the news media so that our military is not compromised." (Owls Head, Maine.)

"Stick to your guns regarding the press. We DON'T 'need to know' about overt operations to any degree that endangers the lives of our service personnel." (Pensacola, Fla.)

"I'm watching today's press briefing and I find the moronic questions and the self-importance of several of the members of the press to be astounding." (Girard, Ohio.)

The Pentagon was riding high. But it would not be long before the downside of the Pentagon's restrictive policy bore fruit.

The Nov. 12 issue of *The New Yorker* carried a scathing account of the Oct. 20 mission written by investigative reporter Seymour M. Hersh, winner of a Pulitzer Prize in 1970 for exposing the My Lai massacre of civilians by U.S. troops in Vietnam.

Hersh reported that, far from encountering "light resistance" as Gen. Myers had described it in his morning-after briefing, the elite Delta Force had been surprised by a fierce firefight, and the Taliban had wounded 12 commandos, three seriously.

It "scared the crap out of everyone," Hersh quoted a senior military officer as saying. According to his account, Delta Force members were complaining that in the raid on Mullah Omar's complex, almost everything went wrong. Pentagon officials denied there was anything more than bruises and scratches suffered by U.S. troops, and insisted none of the injuries were the result of enemy fire.

Some aspects of Hersh's story seemed self-evidently wrong. "The mission was initiated by 16 AC-130 gunships," Hersh wrote, but as veteran *Washington Times* defense correspondents Bill Gertz and Rowan Scarborough pointed out in their "Inside the Ring" column a few days later, "There are only 21 of the aircraft in the entire Air Force inventory." *The Times* quoted military sources as saying, "the Pentagon would never send nearly the entire fleet to one war theater."

But Hersh stuck to his guns, defending the story in a series of interviews, and to some Pentagon critics the account seemed to have an irresistible ring of truth to it. There were, after all, no independent accounts from reporters at or near the action to refute it.

The reason for that, the Pentagon argued, was that the global war on terrorism was a new kind of war that required new tactics, a war in which some parts would be visible, and other parts invisible.

Another concern was operational security. The Pentagon has a very poor record of keeping military operations secret, especially if they involve the movement of large numbers of troops, or hard-to-hide weapons platforms, such as aircraft carriers.

The day of the October raid, Rumsfeld was annoyed that during a visit to Whiteman Air Force Base he was badgered by reporters about a front-page story in *The Washington Post* headlined,

"Special Forces Open Ground Campaign."

The lead of the *Post* report read, "U.S. Special Forces have begun the ground phase of America's war against terrorism in Afghanistan, operating in small numbers in southern Afghanistan in support of the CIA's effort in the Taliban heartland."

For this story to appear while U.S. troops were still on the ground infuriated Rumsfeld.

"The fact that some members of the press knew enough about those operations to ask the questions and to print the stories was clearly because someone in the Pentagon had provided them that information. And clearly, it put at risk the individuals involved in the operation," Rumsfeld said afterward.

The news of the actual raid was first reported by CBS National Security Correspondent David Martin, just after 6:30 p.m. Eastern Time, while the operation was still under way. "We can now report that American commandos are in the midst of their first raid into Taliban-held territory inside Afghanistan. Somewhere between 100 and 200 U.S. Army Rangers have gone in to attack a target that belongs to the Taliban," Martin told Dan Rather in a live report. "We've been asked not to identify the exact target until all of the planes that will bring the Rangers out, all of the aircraft, have left Afghanistan's air space," Martin said.

Leaking classified information is a pet peeve of Rumsfeld's, and during his tenure he has been on a continuing campaign to scare Pentagon officials and military officers into complete silence when it comes to military operations.

But it could be argued there was a much simpler and more effective way to keep such sensitive information out of *The Washington Post*: invite their reporter along. There is no faster way to sensitize a news organization, broadcast or print, to the dangers of reporting too much information than to assign one of their reporters, producers, or camerapersons to a combat unit.

Veteran war correspondent Joseph L. Galloway, co-author of the book, *We Were Soldiers Once…and Young*, tells the story of how, about two weeks before the start of the ground assault in the 1991 Persian Gulf War, he was brought in on the war plan by Maj. Gen. Barry McCaffrey, then commander of the Army's 24th Infantry Division.

"Gen. McCaffrey…called me into his TOC—his tactical operations center—and he pulled the cover off his battle map and he said, 'Here's where we're going.' And I'm looking up there counting Republican Guard divisions and we're going behind them, and the hair is standing up on the back of my neck. And he said, 'I trust you because Schwarzkopf trusts you, but more than that, I trust you because you're coming with me.' And it is the most cogent argument for operational security I've ever heard in my life."

In the early stages of the Afghanistan war, the Pentagon insisted it simply wasn't practical to allow reporters, even in very small numbers, access to special operations forces in the field.

The Americans were operating in small units, typically comprised of Army Special Forces with at least one Air Force forward air controller to call in pinpoint strikes.

A big part of the problem, according to accounts from military officials and journalists alike, is the secretive ethos of the special operations community, who believe nothing good can ever come of discussing or disclosing anything about how they perform their missions.

But there were also plenty of snafus with reporters assigned to regular units. Despite all the advances in videophone and satellite communications technology, Pentagon reticence and lack of planning thwarted reporters on the first day of air strikes, Oct. 7. Reports from television correspondents, including CNN's Walter Rodgers, aboard the U.S. aircraft carrier *Carl Vinson*, didn't air until as much as 20 hours later.

"The Navy locked us down and we could not file live," Rodgers grumbled when he finally got on the air the next day.

Rodgers was also among the 12 pool reporters at Camp Rhino who were confined to a warehouse when U.S. casualties from a Dec. 4 friendly-fire incident were evacuated to the Marine base south of Kandahar. The Pentagon later apologized for denying access and promised to do better, but Rodgers, a veteran of Israeli and Soviet military operations, remained critical of the tight restrictions imposed by the U.S. military. "We had greater freedom of coverage of Soviet military operations in Afghanistan than we had at Camp Rhino," said Rodgers in a *Washington Post* interview after the incident. Reporters at the base were not even allowed to say they were at Camp Rhino.

Even reporters who were intrepid enough to get to Afghanistan on their own, and who did not expect assistance from American troops, found themselves frustrated by the U.S. military. One reporter for a major newspaper chain described how his access to the war zone was often blocked by local Afghan forces who told him they were under orders from U.S. Special Forces to keep any American reporters away from their operations.

"The most beneficial exchange I had with the U.S. Army," the reporter cracked upon his return, "was when I exchanged a case of wine for a case of MREs."

After weeks of complaints from Pentagon reporters and their bureau chiefs about lack of access, the Pentagon did finally arrange for a select group of Pentagon reporters to spend a few days with Special Forces units in Afghanistan at the end of December and beginning of January, but by that time most of the fighting had ended.

The reporters hiked through the rugged Tora Bora Mountains accompanying the U.S. troops as they searched about a dozen cave sites for Osama bin Laden and other Al Qaeda fugitives.

The patrols found only ammunition dumps and documents, but the deployment did demonstrate the feasibility of allowing some reporters along on even the most sensitive missions.

By March, when the U.S. military was gearing up for a major offensive against a concentration of Taliban and Al Qaeda in the Shah-e-kot valley, more regular army troops had joined the fight, and the Pentagon, for the first time in the war, planned to send reporters into battle along with combat troops.

For CNN, the assignment fell to Martin Savidge, a veteran correspondent, who up to then had been cooling his heels at the U.S. base in Kandahar, unable to get permission to accompany troops on even the most routine patrols. For six weeks, Savidge was reduced to reporting features on camp life, while the war waged around him, tantalizingly out of reach.

"We became very frustrated, and I think there was a program where I came on the air and expressed it rather vehemently," Savidge said. "We knew that there was a lot going on, that there were missions going on every day, and that there were important developments that we couldn't bring to you," he said in an interview with CNN after his return.

That changed one day when a public affairs officer came up to Savidge and said, "Why don't we go look at the mountains?" Away from the other reporters, Savidge was informed of the upcoming Operation Anaconda and told he would be the television pool representative. Sworn to secrecy, Savidge couldn't even tell CNN what was up.

Savidge and his cameraman Scottie McWhinnie were flown to Bagram Air Base in the middle of the night and hustled into a command tent, where laid out on the floor was a recreation of the entire Shah-e-kot valley constructed with clay models, with all the objectives marked.

"It's when we looked at that and saw all the objectives out

there that we realized this was going to be the biggest military operation of the war so far in Afghanistan."

There was never any question that CNN would report anything that would remotely jeopardize this mission.

After a harrowing helicopter ride on a CH-47, Savidge and McWhinnie spent several days and bone-chilling nights on the ground, in the line of fire, with the troops. His pool reports, and McWhinnie's footage from the battlefield, provided CNN and other television networks with some of the most riveting coverage of the war.

In a war the Pentagon boasted employed innovative tactics and imaginative doctrine, it should not have taken five months to get a first-hand report from American correspondents on the front lines. But because each war has a fresh batch of military and civilian leaders, these lessons about the value of a free press have to be learned anew in each conflict. "The first casualty when war comes is truth," is the famous quote attributed to California Sen. Hiram W. Johnson at the outbreak of World War I. From my experience, I would say the first casualty is often access, with the result being truth is that much harder to find.

Today's senior military leaders, many of whom served as junior officers in Vietnam, should have learned from experience that the most fair, balanced and truthful coverage comes when news reporters share the battlefield with the combatants.

As Joe Galloway, who covered wars from Vietnam to the Persian Gulf, put it recently, "We did our job, and I think we did it well. I think that remains, for me, the model that should be the goal in military and media relations: honest, open coverage."

Chapter 9
The Relationship After Sept. 11:
A Military View

Brig. Gen. Andrew B. Davis, Director of Public Affairs for the U.S. Marine Corps (USMC), wrote the following from the perspective of the uniformed military. A reserve officer, Davis is Director of Seminars and New Product Development at the Media Management Center at Northwestern University in civilian life. His Pentagon office was destroyed by the terrorist attack on Sept. 11.

O n the night of Nov. 25, 2001, Brig. Gen. James Mattis, of the United States Marine Corps, summoned five reporters to a classified briefing with his unit commanders on board his amphibious ready group flag ship somewhere in the north Arabian Sea.

"Tomorrow," said Mattis, commander of the Marine Corps-Navy task force, "you will be going into Afghanistan with the Marines."

The launch of 1,200 Marines 400 miles into landlocked Afghanistan would be the first introduction of conventional ground forces into the war on terrorism and would signal the first time in the conflict that journalists, print and broadcast, would be embedded with combat troops in the theater of war. That embedding would culminate three weeks of top-level deliberations at the Pentagon and signal a shift in relations between the media, the military, and its civilian leadership since the attacks of Sept. 11.

Early on as the war clouds were darkening, Defense Secretary Donald Rumsfeld assumed the role of lead spokesman for the Department of Defense and the centralized disseminator of information on military action in all theaters. A charismatic, tough and engaging personality, he quickly became the image for the American public, through the media, of the nation's resolve in prosecuting the war against terrorism. His daily briefings, and sparring with the Pentagon press corps, became popular fare with the television viewing audience. Moreover, he emphatically stated, "We will not lie to the American people," an unequivocal stand that was a clear message to press and press officer alike.

The centralization of information flow had a downside as well. It engendered an early friction with Pentagon correspondents and national media. They were more accustomed to open access and the Gulf War model of battlefield information emanating from the theater Commander-in-Chief (CINC). For information and story ideas on the preparations for war, the press turned to the individual service public affairs officers, who were more than glad to oblige. The airways and news pages filled with images and stories on the capabilities of the services, training exercises and modern military equipment. Reporters hit the beaches of Camp Lejeune with Marines, observed carrier operations at sea, flew in Air Force jets, and stalked the woods with Army Rangers. American audiences became reacquainted with their hometown warriors.

That was to change, however, when the campaign against Al Qaeda and the Taliban was launched in October. From the outset, this was clearly going to be a new kind of war, an unconventional war, a truly global conflict with unprecedented global media attention—a war in which a technologically enabled press corps would not have to rely on the permission of the military to transmit its stories. Christiane Amanpour (CNN's Chief International Correspondent), with her satellite videophone, was waiting in Afghanistan for the combatants. And, it soon became apparent that this would be a conflict where journalists would be in harm's way. The first eight casualties of the Afghan war were journalists. The result was tension between the military and the media.

Tension between the two camps is nothing new. In his regulations for war correspondents in 1944, Gen. Dwight D. Eisenhower wrote: "The first essential in military operations is that no information of value should be given to the enemy. The first essential in newspaper work and broadcasting is wide-open publicity. It is your job and mine to try to reconcile these sometime-diverse considerations."

The tension came to a head on Oct. 19, when Army Rangers conducted a night raid into the residential compound of Mullah Mohammed Omar, the ruling cleric of the Taliban. By the next morning, with the ubiquity of press in theater and the instantaneous nature of communications, news of the raid was on the wires. The Pentagon declined to comment on the media reports. The operation was still ongoing. The Pentagon press corps were incensed.

To clear the air, on the following Monday morning, Assistant Secretary of Defense for Public Affairs Victoria Clarke convened a meeting of the Washington bureau chiefs. They were steamed, and for a half hour vented their pique, at which point Kim Hume, Washington Bureau Chief for Fox News, chimed in with a suggestion. The transcript of the exchange follows:

Hume: Would you ever consider doing, when there is something like this, telling us that it's going to happen and telling us that it's going to be over on 10 o'clock on Saturday morning and then we can report it? Because it would definitely solve your problem.

Clarke: I'd rather have the problem than telegraph that

we might be doing an operation. I'll take the problem every time over that.

Hume: …people on the ground and reporters reporting it before they're gone because we don't have information from you that they're finished with the…

Clarke: I'm sorry. I thought what you were saying is that we would tell you in advance that something's going to happen, and here's what's going to happen.

Hume: And they'll be finished at 10 o'clock.

Clarke: No. I won't rule it out, but I just can't imagine the circumstances under which we would telegraph what we were doing.

The exchange points to the initial frustration and lack of understanding by senior leaders of the media about the paramount consideration of military operations that success of the mission comes first, and that safety of our warriors is a close second, what the military calls "OPSEC," operational security.

The next challenge to be worked out in the opening days of the war was to resolve the issue of whether or not to activate the national press pool. Exercises had been conducted with military and journalists participating, but for some reason, as Operation Enduring Freedom unfolded, the call to activate the pool never came. Journalists were on their own to get to the theater of operations, and their resourcefulness took many forms, including hiring horseback caravans to cross snow-crusted mountain passes.

Back in the Pentagon, senior leadership wrestled with such questions as whether senior officers were authorized to grant interviews, if names were to be used should reporters be given access to the combatants, and most pressing for the sea services, if and how we would embed journalists with ships at sea and Marine units once engaged in ground combat. Here is where the service cultures on press relations diverged.

The Marine Corps, of which I am director of public affairs, is essentially a service that has had, over the decades, to defend periodically its very existence. Its strategy has been to retain a close connection with the American people through the press in order to maintain popular support. From the First World War to the Gulf War, Marines have embraced the press. The most famous photograph ever taken, the iconic flag-raising on Iwo Jima, would not have been captured had not a platoon of Marines invited Associated Press photographer Joe Rosenthal with them on their patrol up Mount Suribachi. In Desert Storm, at a time when other services were denying press access, the Marine commander in the desert, Gen. Walt Boomer, himself a former director of USMC public affairs, embedded journalists with his ground combat units, and even his forward command post. The result was a disproportionate share of the credit to the Marines for the retaking of Kuwait, when the actual point of main effort of the campaign was the Army's sweeping flanking movement.

Those lessons are not lost on Marines. When Army soldiers were only giving the first names to press interviewers, and Air Force officers giving call signs, Marines were directed to give their first names and last, and their hometowns, retaining the link with the American public as hometown warriors, not cartoon-like characters with identifiers like "Sgt. Bob" or "Capt. Tom" or "Wingman" or "Acer." With our Navy public affairs counterparts, we worked hard to gain DOD permission first to embed journalists on our warships in the North Arabian Sea, then to have them go forward with the Marine Expeditionary Units on their assault from the sea 400 miles into landlocked Afghanistan. After weeks of discussion, that permission was granted. We swiftly dispatched two officers forward to Bahrain and to the Navy Amphibious Ready Group to augment in-theater public affairs officers. They became the gatekeepers and transportation-enablers for correspondents on their journey to the front.

On the first night of strike operations, 39 correspondents from 26 media organizations were aboard four Navy ships involved in the operation. The media included 12 U.S. television networks or news-papers and 14 international media outlets. When Marines launched their conventional warfare forces into Afghanistan, the five jour-nalists briefed by Brig. Gen. Mattis were along for the 400-mile flight into the combat base, code-named "Rhino." Shortly thereafter, an aircraft brought in 15 additional journalists when a desert airstrip was established. It was not a "pool," per se, rather an informal arrangement that enabled story and equipment sharing. Represented were CNN, *The Washington Post, Los Angeles Times, Wall Street Journal, USA Today,* AP print and film, Agence France Presse, Reuters and the *Times* of London. Within 10 days, the "pool" had filed 177 stories and images of Marines in combat ric-ocheted around the world.

The process was not without its own tensions, problems and missteps. On the night of Dec. 4, U.S. bombs fell short near Kandahar, killing and injuring 24 U.S. and anti-Taliban Afghan sol-diers. Marine and Air Force helicopters evacuated the casualties to Rhino. In an oddity of war, the medevac operations coincided with the inbound flight of a replacement pool of journalists. With the con-fusion and intensity of the casualty-handling operation, suddenly the three press officers on the ground had to contend with 30 journal-ists in two groups, all clamoring for access to the casualties. Their response was to "herd" the reporters away from the scene (a breach of agreed-upon ground rules), restrict them to a central compound of the base, then hustle the outbound group aboard the waiting C-17 airplane, which, it turned out, did not return them to Bahrain as thought, rather to Oman. They were confined to a room for the bet-ter part of a day because they lacked entry visas for that country. The result was a brief flurry of press indignation and hyperbole about the "lockdown," a scathing "Reporter's Notebook" op ed column in *The*

Washington Post, and an apology from Assistant Secretary Clarke.

But the lessons were learned. We augmented the public affairs officer staff in Afghanistan, renegotiated improved ground rules, and put extra effort into enabling the media pools to have access to the Marines. By the time the Marines left Afghanistan in mid-February, the story count was more than 400. When the Army launched Operation Anaconda to root out Al Qaeda remnants from the caves of Tora Bora a month later, they borrowed from the Marines' page. Media were embedded, the Army authorized the use of names, and senior officers on the ground were permitted to give interviews. Friction still existed over prohibited press access to covert, unconventional special operations forces. A *St. Louis Post-Dispatch* story told of the experience of a *New York Times* reporter/photographer team and AP reporter who came across a group of Afghan tribal fighters in the cave region. The Afghan warriors leveled their weapons at the journalists, held them at gunpoint for an hour and confiscated their cameras and film, all while Army Special Forces soldiers looked on. Juxtaposed in the *Post-Dispatch's* story was the account of a contrasting treatment of the media. On the same day the *Times* team was detained, the *Wall Street Journal* ran a front page story about a Marine sniper, "one of the most cold-blooded jobs in the military," the paper said. But, in the words of the *Post-Dispatch,* "neither the Marine nor the *Journal* expressed qualms." The *Journal* printed his full name and hometown and included a line drawing of his face.

For the conventional units, media relations had improved and a better working model for future relations had been crafted. For unconventional forces for whom stealth and secrecy are mission-essential, and often the difference between life and death, achieving a balance with the press is still elusive.

A potential source of conflict between the government and the media was averted in late February 2002, when Rumsfeld emphatically killed the fledgling Pentagon Office of Strategic Influence, a notional department with the prospective mission of coordinating information operations (IO). IO encompasses activities ranging from dropping leaflets and hacking adversaries' computers to propaganda and the dissemination of false information overseas. Defense and service public affairs officers expressed their concern that disinformation in the international arena would taint them in their relations with the press, a relationship forged on trust that the truth is being told. With global communications and the speed of the Internet, an untruth told on foreign shore is likely to ricochet back to the domestic front instantly. "The lesson," said Clarke, "is what a lot of us have known for a long time, that truth is always the best weapon...."

We've looked at lessons learned from the military perspective. What, from that same viewpoint, can the press do better? Three suggestions:

1. Develop a better understanding of and appreciation for the need for operational security. Mission does come first for the warriors in uniform, and safety of those warriors is close behind. Admittedly, most leaks come not from operating forces but from sources near the top. Case in point: an early July 2002 story in the *New York Times* outlining U.S. war plans for the invasion of Iraq. In the words of Rumsfeld, the leaking of such information "is wrong. It's against the law. It costs the lives of Americans. It diminishes our country's chance for success."

2. Become knowledgeable about the military and military operations. With the passing of the draft and universal service in the early 1970s, few journalists have military experience. The resulting errors in reporting by inexperienced journalists, missed by editors who lack military knowledge, diminish respect for the media in the eyes of their military sources. For example, military readers derided an otherwise strong *Washington Post* profile of FBI Director Robert

Mueller that recounted that Mueller had served as a Marine officer in Vietnam where "he won the Bronze Medal." There is a huge distinction between the Bronze Star Medal for valor in combat, and the award for third place in a sporting contest. The *Post's* military reporting credibility was diminished by the error.

3. Build relationships with military sources. The best reporting comes from solid information from reliable sources. When a tribal conflict of cultures exists, that information will not be forthcoming. In the hallways of the Pentagon, I know whom I can trust with background information, who will get the story right. They will get the story first from me. The same exists on the battlefield.

The goal is a relationship of two-way trust, of willingness to share the same fighting hole. Our public affairs officers and most reporters in Afghanistan forged that bond. In mid-January, I received a letter from a *Wall Street Journal* reporter who had spent two months following the Marines in the Persian Gulf and Afghanistan. The purpose of his letter was to express appreciation for the work of the Marines who enabled his coverage. "While there were some well-known bumps in the road for reporters covering the Afghan war," he wrote, "you and several of your men did their utmost to make it possible for me to tell the Marine story. Their help was invaluable, their patience monumental, and their humor virtually inexhaustible…If there is another war, I want to spend it with the Marines."

And I with him. That is the essence of the successful cultivation of media-military relations.

Appendix:
Explanation of Major Incidents

Following are explanations of various incidents referred to in this report.

Tailhook (Robert Stumpf)

At the 1991 convention of the Tailhook Association (an organization of naval aviators), a number of women were assaulted by drunken Navy pilots. Cmdr. Robert E. Stumpf, who was at the convention, was acquitted of wrongdoing by a court of inquiry. But in June 1994, the Senate Armed Services Committee asked the Secretary of the Navy to deny Stumpf's promotion to captain because the Navy had not let them know that he had been investigated for having attended Tailhook. Stumpf resigned from the Navy in October 1996.

USS Greeneville (Scott Waddle)

On Feb. 9, 2001, the *USS Greeneville* surfaced suddenly off the coast of Hawaii, striking and sinking a Japanese fishing boat, the Ehime Maru, and killing nine people. The commander of the nuclear submarine, Scott Waddle, was found guilty of dereliction of duty and negligent hazarding of a vessel. Though Waddle said he was distracted by civilians onboard the submarine, the Navy's investigation determined that they had not directly contributed to the collision. Waddle received a letter of reprimand in April and subsequently retired from the Navy.

Vincennes/Iranian airbus

On July 3, 1988, the *USS Vincennes* mistakenly identified an Iranian Airbus passenger jet for an Iranian fighter plane and shot it down over the Persian Gulf, killing all 290 people aboard. The Pentagon exonerated Capt. Will Rogers of the Navy cruiser, in part because the airliner failed to respond to the *Vincennes'* repeated warnings. Rogers retired honorably in 1991.

Cavalese, Italy, cable car incident (Richard Ashby)

Twenty people were killed on Feb. 3, 1998 in the Italian ski resort town of Cavalese when a U.S. Marines EA-6B prowler jet cut through the wires of a cable car, sending it crashing to the slopes below. The pilot, Capt. Richard J. Ashby, was acquitted of manslaughter by a U.S. military jury but was later sentenced to six months in prison and dismissed from the Marines for destroying a videotape of the flight. The jet's navigator, Capt. Joseph Schweitzer, was also dismissed for destroying the videotape. Charges against two back-seat crewmen were dropped.

Gene McKinney

In 1997, Army Sgt. Maj. Gene McKinney, then the highest-ranking enlisted man in the Army, was accused of sexual misconduct by six female soldiers. In March 1998, a military jury at Fort Belvoir, Va., cleared him of 18 out of 19 counts, convicting him on one count of obstructing justice. McKinney received a reprimand and was demoted to the rank of master sergeant. He retired shortly thereafter.

Annapolis cheating scandal

A total of 134 midshipmen were implicated in the December 1992 cheating scandal at the U.S. Naval Academy in Annapolis, Md. A special naval tribunal found 62 of the midshipmen guilty of honor violations for cheating on an exam and issued punishments short of expulsion. After a 16-month review by Navy Secretary John Dalton, 24 of the midshipmen were ordered expelled.

No Gun Ri Massacre

In September 1999, the Associated Press released a story reporting that U.S. Army soldiers had fired into a crowd of South Korean refugees under a railroad bridge in the vicinity of No Gun Ri in July 1950, killing as many as 300. After a 15-month investigation, the Department of the Army determined that U.S. soldiers had killed or injured an unconfirmed number of Korean refugees.

Apaches in Albania

Twenty-four AH-64 Apache attack helicopters were dispatched to Albania in April 1999 to participate in Operation Allied Force, the ongoing NATO air campaign against Yugoslav forces in Kosovo. Due to serious problems, however, including a lack of adequately trained pilots and two highly publicized training accidents, the second of which resulted in the death of two Army pilots, "Task Force Hawk," as the unit was known, was never employed in combat.

Vieques

Protests against bombing exercises on the Puerto Rican island of Vieques grew after April 19, 1999, when a Navy pilot dropped two bombs from an FA-18 jet that missed their target and killed a civilian security guard. In response to the growing protests, President George Bush announced in June 2001 that the exercises would end. Pentagon officials specified the end date as May 2003 when the current agreement on the range expires.

MV-22 Osprey—maintenance problems; *60 Minutes*

After 23 Marines were killed in two crashes of the U.S. Marine Corps' MV-22 Osprey aircraft in 2000, the news program *60 Minutes* aired an investigative report. During the program, which aired on Jan. 21, 2001, an audiotape was played in which Lt. Col. Fred Leberman, commanding officer of the Osprey Unit in New River, N.C., could be heard instructing his squadron to lie about the safety of the Osprey in order to gain funding for the aircraft. Leberman was relieved of his command in February 2001. Seven other Marines were implicated in the scandal, which included charges of falsification of records, and faced "non-judicial punishment." Flight operations were suspended after the second crash on Dec. 11, 2000, and production of the Osprey was slowed to the minimum.

Gold Wing hazing

In 1997, NBC's *Dateline* aired videos from 1991 and 1993 showing U.S. Marines pounding half-inch-long posts of "Gold Wing" pins into the chests of other Marines. This hazing ritual, called "blood-winging," was for Marines who completed 10 parachute jumps. Marines implicated by the videos received punishments ranging from counseling to discharge. In June 1997, the Marine Corps issued tougher rules against hazing, which specifically banned "rites of passage that are cruel, abusive, humiliating, or oppressive."

Beating of gay soldier at Fort Campbell, Ky.

On July 5, 1999, Pfc. Barry Winchell, a gay soldier with the 101st Airborne Division, Fort Campbell, Ky., was beaten to death with a baseball bat while he slept. A military panel charged Army Pvt. Calvin Glover with premeditated murder. Glover was subsequently sentenced to life in prison. Winchell's roommate, Spec. Justin R. Fisher, was charged as an accomplice and sentenced to 12 and a half years in prison.

Aberdeen

In November 1996, the Army charged 11 drill sergeants with sexual misconduct at the Army's Ordinance Training Center at the Aberdeen Proving Grounds in Maryland. The commander of seven of the accused drill sergeants, Lt. Col. Martin Utzig, was suspended in July 1997. Several of the Aberdeen soldiers were convicted of sexual misconduct or left the Army to avoid court-martial. Letters of reprimand were issued to eight officers and enlisted leaders, virtually ending their careers.

Air Force Senior Officer Travel Abuse

In September 1994, Air Force Gen. Joseph W. Ashy flew on an Air Mobility Command C141-B aircraft from Naples, Italy to Colorado Springs, Co., to assume his new post at U.S. Space Command. Though the only passengers on board were Ashy and an aide, seats were denied to space-available travelers. A report issued by the Department of Defense Inspector General in June 1995 criticized Ashy and identified problems with the way Air Force public affairs officials had handled the matter.

Kelly Flinn

Air Force Lt. Kelly Flinn, the first female B-52 bomber pilot, was accused of having an affair with a married civilian, lying about it to investigators and disobeying an order to end the affair. She was also accused of having a relationship with an enlisted man. She left the service in 1997 after the Secretary of the Air Force offered her a general discharge in lieu of continuing court martial proceedings.

Andrew J. Bacevich
Boston University

John W. Bergman
U.S. Marine Corps

Tom Bowman
The Baltimore Sun

Kevin P. Byrnes
U.S. Army

Tony Capaccio
Bloomberg News

James Carmichael
U.S. Coast Guard

James E. Cartwright
U.S. Marine Corps

Sig Christenson
San Antonio Express-News

John D. W. Corley
U.S. Air Force

Bantz J. Craddock
U.S. Army

James Crawley
The San Diego Union-Tribune

Philip J. Crowley
Insurance Information
Institute, New York

Andrew Davis
U.S. Marine Corps

Pat Dickson
European and Pacific Stars and Stripes

Harry Disch
Center for Media
and Security

Bill Douglas
Newsday

Kevin Eldridge
U.S. Coast Guard

Thomas Fargo
U.S. Navy

Bill Gertz
Washington Times

Timothy W. Ghormley
U.S. Marine Corps

Charles W. Gittins
Attorney, Middletown, Va.

Tom Gjelten
National Public Radio

Michael A. Hamel
U.S. Air Force

John Hawkins III
U.S. Army

Charles Henry
WTOP-FM/AM

Greg Jaffe
Wall Street Journal

Jason K. Kamiya
U.S. Army

Timothy J. Keating
U.S. Navy

James Kitfield
National Journal

Jonathan Landay
Knight-Ridder Newspapers,
Washington, D.C.

T.L. McCreary
U.S. Navy

Jamie McIntyre
Cable News Network

Duncan McNabb
U.S. Air Force

John Needham, Jr.
Los Angeles Times

Stephen R. Pietropaoli
U.S. Navy

Craig R. Quigley
U.S. Navy

Steve Ramsey
Tribune Television

Ronald T. Rand
U. S. Air Force

Dennis J. Reimer
U.S. Army (Ret.)

Rick Rogers
Daily Press,
Newport News, Va.

Jim Schwenk
Department of Defense

Ivan Scott
WTOP Federal News Radio,
Washington, D.C.

Thom Shanker
New York Times

Jeffrey H. Smith
Arnold & Porter,
Washington, D.C.

Barbara Starr
ABC News

James Stavridis
U.S. Navy

Michael B. Suessmann
Department of
Defense (Ret.)

Mark Thompson
Time

Vivian E. Vahlberg
McCormick Tribune
Foundation

Robert Wall
*Aviation Week &
Space Technology*

Mary Walsh
CBS News

Frank Wolfe
Defense Daily, Arlington, Va.